CONFRONTING
reality

LARRY BOSSIDY

and

RAM CHARAN

with Charles Burck

CONFRONTING reality

Doing What

Matters to Get

Things Right

RANDOM HOUSE
BUSINESS BOOKS

First published in the UK in 2004 by Random House Business Books,
Random House, 20 Vauxhall Bridge Road, London SW1V 2SA

Random House Australia (Pty) Limited
20 Alfred Street, Milsons Point
Sydney, New South Wales 2061, Australia

Random House New Zealand Limited
18 Poland Road, Glenfield
Auckland 10, New Zealand

Random House (Pty) Limited
Endulini, 5a Jubilee Road, Parktown 2193, South Africa

The Random House Group Limited Reg. No. 954009

Papers used by Random House are natural, recyclable products made
from wood grown in sustainable forests. The manufacturing processes
conform to the environmental regulations of the country of origin.

ISBN 1 8441 3689 2

Companies, institutions and other organizations wishing to make
bulk purchases of books published by Random House should contact
their local bookstore or Random House direct:
Special Sales Director
Random House, 20 Vauxhall Bridge Road, London SW1V 2SA

Tel 020 7840 8470 Fax 020 7828 6681

www.randomhouse.co.uk
businessbooks@randomhouse.co.uk

Printed and bound in the United Kingdom by
Mackays of Chatham plc, Chatham, Kent

Contents

Contents

Introduction

Breaking with the Past

It's time to radically change the way you think about your business.

Any plan for a business has to answer three questions: What's the nature of the game we're in? Where is it going? How do we make money in it? These questions go to the heart of what business is all about; they are the fundamentals of business thinking. Yet–incredibly–in many organizations today they rarely get asked, much less answered, adequately.

It takes unflinching realism to get such answers. But the established methodologies for defining the purpose of a business and planning its future have drifted steadily away from realism. Many people in business today are boxed in by dysfunctional practices and habits that more often than not obscure reality, rather than expose it. Many have succeeded anyway in the past. Fewer will in the future, because–as we will see shortly–the business environment is becoming far less forgiving of mistakes.

When we wrote *Execution* almost three years ago, we focused on the gap between strategic plans and their outcomes, which so often fall short of the planners' ambitions. We pinpointed execution as the missing element, and explained how to link the strategy, operations and budgeting, and people processes to achieve effective results. This was

1

a reality-based approach and we've been gratified by the number of people who've used its lessons to improve their businesses.

But it turns out that we'd only begun our journey. As we continued with the thinking we'd started, we dug deeper into the reasons for our own successes and failures along with those of others whom we'd known and observed. Eventually we found that the gap originates with the very nature of how people conceive the purpose and direction of their businesses.

In many organizations, large and small, the process is flawed. People don't fully understand the game they're playing because they don't look at it hard enough. They don't ask whether they can realistically make the money they hope to, and why. Specifically, they don't analyze and link the three fundamental components that determine a business's success or failure: the environment it operates in, the financial targets it needs to meet, and the internal activities and capabilities that it depends on in the given environment to meet the financial targets.

Why not? Because until now there hasn't been a specific discipline for understanding the game at this level. The traditional strategic planning process is an approximation, but it falls short because it doesn't force people to organize the fundamental components into a framework that links them rigorously.

Everyone needs to fully understand the realities of the world in which they do business, and they need a new way to mesh their business goals and actions with those realities. We show how to do this with a specific and unique methodology using a concept that is widely misunderstood: the business model.

"Business model" is a new name for an ancient analytical tool. The people who succeed in business at any level, from shopkeepers in primitive third-world villages to entrepreneurs drawing up their first business plans to CEOs of global corporations, have always worked with business models, most of them intuitive. Today spreadsheets allow you to construct highly elaborate models, but the basic premise hasn't changed: a business model makes it possible for you to gain a comprehensive and realistic understanding of how to make money.

The version of the business model we have developed is a robust, reality-based process for thinking about the speciWcs of your business in a holistic way. It shows you how to tie together the financial targets you must meet, the external realities of your business and internal activities including strategy, operating activities, selection and development of people, and organizational processes and structure.

Our business model builds realism into the process of plotting your company's direction by enabling you to link specific facts about the external environment with your financial aims, organizational capabilities, and action plans. It tells you sooner rather than later when your fundamental business premise is under assault, where your best opportunities lie, and whether you need to change internal activities or the business model itself. It will be your central tool for confronting reality.

The fact is that the strategic plans of most companies don't work. A key reason why is that little time, if any, is spent harmonizing the facts of the external environment, the financial targets that are set and the internal capabilities of the business so that these discrete activities work together. Let's say, for example, that one of your financial targets is 12 percent sales growth, but that the overall growth of your served market is 5 percent. Without specific programs dedicated to meeting that top line objective–marketing, sales incentives, the right people in the right jobs, et cetera–the 12 percent goal is a chimera and the likelihood of the strategy working is close to zero.

Your business model is incomplete and ineffective unless you debate and harmonize your external environment and financial targets with your internal capabilities through a process we call "iteration." As we will show throughout the book, iteration is not a one-shot meeting that gathers up key people for a review, but a mentally challenging recurring activity to get things right. Once you start to practice it you've confronted reality and built a platform for profitability, growth, and prosperity in synch with what is going on in the world.

The process of iteration makes you confront the world the way it really is, not how you would like it to be. It is intimately tied to the idea of "business savvy." People often use the phrase to describe really astute business leaders, the kind of people who possess a shrewd, instinctual feel about how to make money. Business savvy distinguishes those who over time consistently make their businesses succeed from those who have the occasional stroke of genius or lucky break.

Our analysis of business savvy shows that its essence is the use, intuitively or explicitly, of the business model in choosing where and how to make money. People with business savvy have specific financial targets in their minds. These targets are the reference point for everything they do, from looking for opportunities and dangers in the external environment to designing the combination of strategies, operating practices, people, and organizational processes that will enable them to capitalize on the opportunities and avoid the dangers. And guess what? People with a well-developed sense of business savvy seldom have a strategy ahead of time. Instead, they devise their strategies as a means of meeting their financial targets, not the other way around. How they do this is a point we will develop at length and illustrate through analysis of companies in a wide range of businesses.

What kind of people are we talking about? Sam Walton, Michael Dell, Jack Welch, the successful proprietor of a shoe store in Bombay . . . and, would you believe Billy Beane, general manager of the Oakland A's?

In Major League Baseball, as everyone knows, the rich keep getting richer and the poor get poorer. Teams in big markets will always be able to outspend those in smaller ones because they have more revenues. Who can compete with Yankees' owner George Steinbrenner's vast treasure chest in hiring talent? The Yankees, along with teams in big metropolitan markets like the Boston Red Sox and the Los Angeles Dodgers, have framed a business model based on rich television and radio revenues that provide them with pots of money to bid for highly regarded players.

Oakland is a small-market team supposedly doomed to also-ran status. And yet with one of the lowest payrolls in baseball, Billy Beane defied conventional wisdom in one of the most tradition-bound of businesses and created one of the winningest records of the past several years.

As related in Michael Lewis's book *Moneyball,* Beane discovered the reality that more than a century of conventional wisdom about the basics of the baseball business was wrong. He questioned traditional criteria used to judge the value of players such as batting average, runs batted in, and home runs. They didn't correlate, he observed, with the actual value of the contributions players made to teams. Beane began using new criteria for measuring the skills of ballplayers. For example, the ability to get on base turned out to be a crucial component of scoring runs. The ability of a batter to take a deep ball-and-strike count—that is, handle the bat with enough skill to keep the pitcher throwing as many pitches as possible—both raised the chance of getting on base and helped wear the pitcher down.

Scouting players using the new fact-based criteria, Beane was able to assemble a team of affordable players undervalued by traditional measures.

In business terms, Beane had the business savvy to recognize that structural change in the baseball industry had put his organization at a disadvantage. Instead of entering a losing battle by trying to figure out different strategies for success using players selected on the old criteria, as other small-market teams were doing, he rethought the very basis of success. In essence, he designed a new business model that created fundamental value for the Oakland franchise.

■ ■ ■

LIKE OTHER PEOPLE with business savvy, Billy Beane confronted the reality of his situation. To confront reality is to recognize the world as it is, not as you wish it to be, and have the courage to do what must be done, not what you'd like to do.

It never has been easy to face reality; there are a plethora of psychological reasons why people in all areas of life, not just business, shrink from it. But the price of unrealistic business thinking is rapidly heading upward, because the game is going into uncharted territory.

Everyone senses that business conditions are different from those of a few years ago, yet few grasp just how fundamental the changes are and how swiftly they are overtaking businesses of all kinds. The business environment has changed by an order of magnitude.

The economy appeared back on growth track as we went to press. More and more businesses were looking for ways to grow, innovate, and generally become bolder. The recovery could get derailed, of course, but let's assume it's still rolling at the time you're reading our book. The fact remains that any good times from now on won't look like the good times of years past.

Globalization is now a force that touches all businesses, even those that once seemed too specific, local, or small to worry about it. One reason is the Internet, which speeds decision making and the flow of ideas radically, linking all areas of the world into a real-time network. Another is the vast credit expansion of the recent past. Immense and highly mobile flows of capital have created worldwide overinvestment, along with overcapacity in industries from autos to consumer electronics to software. Together, these forces have helped to create a global buyer's market. The result is one of the biggest changes in business history: an unprecedented shift of power from the owners and managers of capital to consumers and intermediaries, including especially giant retailers such as Wal-Mart.

Global cost parity is becoming everybody's benchmark. New and unexpected competition can come from anywhere. New products become commodities almost overnight. Lack of pricing power and relentless pressure on profit margins will continue to haunt businesses, regardless of whether the economy is weak or strong.

These changes have the potential to obliterate your business—or to take it to an entirely new level. Which will it be? That largely depends on how realistically you understand your position in the ever-shifting business environment and translate that understanding into your financial goals and action plans.

Regardless of whether you are being hit by these changes today or in the longer term, the imperative is to recognize the position of your business and take action. Acting in anticipation of what is on the horizon can bring enormous rewards; waiting too long to initiate action eliminates many of your options.

Leaders with business savvy confront reality as a matter of course. It's often said that business savvy is inherent; it's part of a person's genetic makeup. Some people are indeed born with it (we know a number of them personally). But we believe it can be developed by just about any good businessperson.

Business savvy is the art of understanding the fundamentals driving your business and the connections among them. This is precisely what our business model enables you to do. It gives you a new way to develop an integrated picture of your business reality, calculated at the very beginning of any effort to plan your course and recalculated regularly as circumstances change. The picture of reality will enable you to answer the following questions:

- Is the how of making money in my business and industry changing?
- Who is winning in my industry, who is not winning, and why?
- How, specifically, are the winners making money?
- If my business is a winner, what do I need to do to stay on top?
- Conversely, if I need to change my game, what, specifically, should I be doing?
- Am I in a growth industry or not? If not, and I want to continue playing in the game, how do I change it or play it better than the competition?
- Is my organization moving quickly to spot and take advantage of growth opportunities generated by these changes?

Some people try to fend off disruptive forces of change by denouncing or ignoring them. But in this new environment, confronting reality has to become a leadership priority of the highest order–a nonnegotiable behavior for everyone at all levels of an organization.

Plenty of savvy businesspeople around the world *are* willing to try something different. As a result, we predict, most businesses will be required to change more and more often in the coming decade than they have in their previous histories. And if they stick with their old practices and behaviors, a great many won't be able to handle the changes.

That doesn't mean that everybody will have to be

changing everything all the time. We don't agree with the gurus who insist that revolution and reinvention have to be part of the daily leadership agenda. Knowing what to change and what *not* to change will be another important challenge in this turbulent era. This you can know only by confronting reality with a rigorous business model.

We start in Part I, "Why Confront Reality," by explaining the forces of change that are permanently altering many industries. Part II, "Confronting Reality with the Business Model," explains the workings of our business model and illustrates how business-savvy leaders have used its principles.

Part III, "What to Change and What Not to Change," shows how EMC, Cisco, Home Depot, 3M, and The Thomson Corporation used the business model framework to decide what they needed to change—and what could be left alone. And Part IV, "How to Prepare for Change," provides insight into how you should anticipate future events, how to condition your culture for the changes required and, most important, how to develop the leaders who can succeed in this tumultuous environment. We conclude with a letter to our friend Jane, a business unit manager facing both danger and opportunity, with some ideas about how she and her team can better meet the challenge of structural change.

Now go forth and confront reality.

part I

Why Confront Reality

Whether change is abrupt or gradual, at some point it makes old beliefs and behaviors obsolete. Ignoring that reality, as so many leaders do, is devastating. We've seen people fail to grasp that they can no longer earn a decent living in their business, let alone grow sales in the double digits, or that their products will never again have the pricing power they once had. We've also seen people to whom change presented wonderful growth opportunities that they missed because they weren't paying attention to the changes going on around them.

Though businesspeople like to think of themselves as realists, the fact is that wishful thinking, denial, and other forms of avoiding reality are deeply embedded in most corporate cultures. But what's been tolerated in the past can't be tolerated in this new environment. The price for failing to confront reality is simply too high.

Globalization is an old idea but we are only beginning to see what radical and pervasive changes it is bringing. The integration of business activity across borders, which the Internet has accelerated by an order of magnitude, means that virtually every business is now playing in a global game. New competitors can come from anywhere. Cost benchmarks are set wherever in the world somebody can produce something most cheaply. At the same time, the vast credit expansion of the past decade and immense flow of risk capital have created worldwide overinvestment. Finally, powerful retailers such as Wal-Mart and Home Depot are calling more and more of the shots in the demand chain.

In short, we're in a new business era. It is the fifth distinct era of structural change since the end of World War II. Each of the previous ones spawned new management theories and practices, and this one will be no exception: the old ways don't work in this age of lightning-fast change, high volatility, hypercompetition, declining prices, and compressed margins. The tools, practices, and behaviors that will distinguish success from failure can be summed up in one phrase: relentless realism.

CHAPTER 1

When Reality Bites: The Stories of John P. and Lou G.

The most widespread unrealistic behavior when the game changes drastically is to violate the First Law of Holes (when you're in one, stop digging). People redouble their efforts to do what they know best. They often achieve heroic results—which are, alas, almost as often pointless, because they fail to confront the new realities.

For example, many managers facing competition from abroad are still fighting yesterday's war. That's the one the Japanese started with their efficient manufacturing processes. Today even the Japanese can't win it. Doubling your productivity is a wonderful accomplishment, but it does not confront reality because it won't save you when your competitors have global supply chains with costs that are a small fraction of what you can hope to achieve in your home country. Services are now in the equation too. Customer support, back-office operations, product development, and even some segments of R&D can be as outsourceable as factories.

Consider John P., a business unit leader we know. In mid-2003, John and his top managers were preparing the 2004 strategic plan for their $500 million division, which made protective coatings for a highly specialized industrial market. John had run the division superbly for more than five years, and was considered a candidate for senior leadership of the parent company. He knew operations, and had good relationships with his customers.

Recently those customers had been telling him that their sales were down because of competition from abroad. They allowed that John's products were the best on the market, but they were under tremendous pressure to reduce their costs, and they expected all their suppliers to do the same. John took their message seriously, and told his people what he'd heard.

John's team agreed they could do a number of things to cut costs. They worked out a plan to close one of their four U.S. plants, consolidate three European plants into two, tighten other expenses wherever they could, and increase R&D spending to further distance their product from the competition's. Based on past experience and on what everyone present at the meeting knew, the plan looked realistic.

Then the new CFO spoke up. He'd joined the company only recently and was seeing the issue from a broader perspective. "From my point of view, you appear to be heading down the wrong track," he said. "Your recommendations would be good if the problem was our traditional domestic competition. They might satisfy the customers in the short term. But I know for a fact that two of those customers have already started moving to China. The others will undoubtedly be doing the same soon. Don't they expect us to reduce our costs just as significantly? Closing a U.S. plant, consolidating in Europe, and cutting costs by a few percentage points won't do that."

John looked around the room and noted that the other members of his team seemed just as discomfited as he felt. "I'm not sure what to do," the CFO continued, "but I urge you to consider the pros and cons of moving the whole operation to China or licensing our technology to a China-based supplier."

John knew that lots of businesses were outsourcing to China these days. Still, the idea stunned him. It just didn't make sense for this company.

"Mike," he said to the CFO. "This is not something we need to do—or even necessarily can do. You surely know that a lot of our differentiation comes from the application process. That's all about proprietary techniques and human experience. How could anybody duplicate that elsewhere?

"But let's suppose we did move production to China. We'd have to take a huge write-off on our plant here. The unions would raise hell. Morale in the whole division would be hurt. And while you can't necessarily take this to the bank, we'd get a huge black eye in the community. I've been part of this town for years, I'm on the school board and coach in the Little League. I don't know how I could look my friends and neighbors in the face if we did this.

"We can cut our costs significantly with our plan. Maybe they won't be as low as they would be in China. But we're the leader in this technology, and that's got to be worth a premium to our customers."

"You could do all the things you plan to do, but they're probably not enough," said the CFO. "Our differentiation is real enough, but frankly it's not worth it to people who can save a lot of money from another supplier. Besides, our customers will expect us to be located in close proximity to their operations. If you don't make the move, they'll sooner or later find somebody who will."

In the quiet that followed, John thought back to something one of his customers had said a few weeks before.

Talking about his costs, the customer had remarked almost casually that he'd reduced a big chunk of them by dropping a longstanding component supplier in favor of one based in China. Could that have been a hint John didn't want to hear? In light of what Mike was saying, it sure looked like one now.

As he pondered, he gazed out the window. The first shift was leaving the plant for the day. He saw the faces of people he knew—guys and gals he'd talked to on the plant floor. They were as dedicated a bunch of workers as you could find anywhere in the world. Many of their kids went to the same school as his kids.

Life really isn't fair, John thought to himself. Nobody should have to make decisions like this. Finally he turned back to the CFO and looked at him bleakly. "Okay," he said. "I hate the idea, but you've convinced me that we'll have to do this at some point. But our current plan will buy us enough time to do that in an orderly fashion—won't it?"

The CFO responded sympathetically but firmly. "Let me rephrase my thoughts," he said. "You're looking at the world from the American Midwest, and you're looking at it as you've seen it for your whole life.

"These days, later is a lot closer to sooner than it used to be. There's big change going on, and it's happening fast because the global economy has gone real-time. It's not cyclical change. It's *structural* change, and it means total change in how this business will make money in the future. By the way, your customer is struggling with similar structural change. And it begins with one simple fact in this case: You've got to have global cost parity, meaning that you cannot be out of line with the lowest-cost source, no matter how fine your product may be.

"Now, you can't just pick up and relocate to China overnight. You've got to integrate vertically, which means not only getting a plant built but getting acclimated to the new environment, selecting suppliers, and picking and training the right people. This requires a knowledge of China, and nobody in this company has it. If you do bite the bullet, you've got a lot of work to do before you even start to build an operation there."

Within a week, John's team had a new message for the CEO. They wouldn't present the strategic plan he was expecting. Instead, they'd be back in six weeks with a fully detailed China proposal—including the names of experts to engage, along with plans and a budget for a new plant and a plan for structuring the necessary write-offs in the United States.

John handed the report over with mixed emotions. He suspected the pain of making the decision would never entirely go away. But he also recognized that he'd been lucky. He and his team thought they were being realistic about their situation, and that they had taken the necessary hard actions to correct it. A person with a fresh viewpoint had shown him realities that would have sunk his business and his career if he hadn't faced up to them.

■ ■ ■

IN THEORY, CONFRONTING REALITY is what business is all about. More than most, businesspeople like to think they're realists. Their actions look like realism: they work hard to gather relevant facts and data, they research alternatives rigorously, and they bring their cumulative knowledge and experience to bear on the issues. They test their thinking in arguments and debates. Then they reach conclusions. Surely, after all this work, the conclusions are realistic.

But the implicit faith in realism is all too often unjustified. Unless you're in a rare organization, you've seen this yourself. In our decades of experience, we've wrestled firsthand with it in hundreds of companies and many industries. The best strategies, the most rigorous research, the clearest of operating plans—all are undermined because the key people behind them have missed the reality of the situation for one reason or another. The fact is that the greatest consistent damage to businesses and their owners is the result not of poor management technique but of the failure, sometimes willful, to confront reality.

BRING REALITY TO IBM

Lou Gerstner's fundamental contribution to IBM was to force reality on a company that had become cripplingly unreal. His autobiography offers a telling portrait of what he found when he arrived in 1993.[1]

When Gerstner took over, the conventional wisdom was that IBM needed to be broken up into smaller companies. In the new, decentralized world of information technology, the reasoning went, new companies with bright ideas and new products were multiplying almost as fast as desktops. CIOs would want to pick and choose the best hardware and software and integrate it into their very own systems. Nobody wanted to deal with yesterday's monolith.

This view was shared by almost everybody in the industry, along with Wall Street's analysts and the business press. It's what investment bankers had urged upon John Akers, Gerstner's predecessor. Akers was starting to put the plan in place, but by then IBM's liquidity and cash position had become so poor that the board began looking for a new CEO.

Gurus were expecting a CEO with a technology background who would take IBM from a mainframe business to one with the PC at the center. To its credit, the board instead chose Gerstner, whose expertise was not in technology but who had superb business savvy, honed through years of experience. Initially a McKinsey consultant, he'd been president of American Express and at the time was CEO of RJR Nabisco.

Gerstner was all but certain that breaking IBM into pieces was the wrong thing to do. He had been an IT customer at RJR Nabisco and American Express, and he knew other customers. All agreed that in the real world of the IT managers, not many wanted to undertake the complex job of cobbling together workable systems from an infinity of vendors. Integration, he wrote, was becoming "a gigantic problem.... I believed there was a very important role for some company to be able to integrate all of the pieces and deliver a working solution to the customer." So he made the decision—a courageous one in the face of universal views to the contrary—to keep the company intact, and to reshape it to deliver just those kinds of solutions.

He traced IBM's financial problems to the mainframe business. IBM's flagship System/390 was being undercut by competing products based on cheaper open-system technology and priced 30 percent to 40 percent less. Because fixed costs were high, the market share losses were rapidly draining cash.

"Why don't we lower our prices?" asked Gerstner. IBM's

executives explained that they needed the profits they were getting from wide margins earned on mainframes. But it was clear to Gerstner that milking System/390 would kill not only the line but also, in all likelihood, IBM itself. It had not occurred to the management team that the company needed the cash more than the profits. After he showed them why, they completely reversed their old beliefs and behaviors. The price cut enabled the mainframe product line to rebound.

Meantime IBM was continuing to pour tens of millions of dollars into developing OS/2, a desktop operating system it had created some years before. OS/2 would have been the natural system for IBM's own PCs, but IBM had chosen instead to use Microsoft's Windows because at the time it wasn't convinced the PC had much of a future. Nevertheless, IBM continued to press on with OS/2 development in an effort to compete with Microsoft. "The highest levels of IBM executives were almost obsessed with the effort to unwind the decisions of the 1980s and take back control of the operating system from Microsoft (and, to a lesser extent, gain control of the microprocessor from Intel)," Gerstner wrote. "Not only were we banging our heads against a very hard, unrelenting wall, but I had to wonder if anyone was paying attention to the strategic direction we were talking about. If we truly believed that the reign of the PC was coming to an end, why were we pouring energy, resources, and our image into yesterday's war? It was counter to our view of where the world was headed."

These were not isolated problems. Unreality at IBM, Gerstner discovered, was systemic and endemic. IBM had all the assets it needed to succeed, Gerstner says. "But in every case—hardware, technology, software, even services—all of these capabilities were part of a business model that had fallen wildly out of step with marketplace realities."

How did this happen? The organization was so focused on processes and turf battles that it was almost oblivious to what its customers wanted. For example, Gerstner recalls his first strategy meeting as possibly the low point of his first year at the company: "While the people in the room were extremely bright, very committed, and, at times, quite convinced of what needed to be done, there was little underpinning for the strategies discussed. Not once was the question of customer segmentation raised. Rarely did we compare our offerings to those of our competitors. There was no integration across the various topics that allowed the group to pull together a total IBM view."

A similar eye-opener was his first meeting with the top-level Management Committee, "the ultimate position of power that every IBM executive aspired to as the apex of his or her career." In the distant past it had been organized as a forum for contention, where staff people would challenge the recommendations of line units. "The problem was that over time, IBM people learned how to exploit the system to promote their own agendas," Gerstner wrote. "So by the early 1990s a system of true contention was apparently replaced by a system of prearranged consensus. Rather than have proposals debated, the corporate staff, without executives, worked out a consensus across the company at the lowest possible level.... Too often the MC's mission was a formality—a rubber-stamp approval."

THE SIX HABITS OF HIGHLY UNREALISTIC LEADERS

If you think the old IBM was unique, you either haven't been working in the corporate world, or you haven't been paying attention to what goes on around, above, and below you.

People often fall short in confronting both their external realities and their internal realities. The external realities generally have to do with the behaviors of others who can affect the business's outcomes: customers and markets; traditional industry competitors or nontraditional competitors (often from completely different industries); policies of governments and regulators; the expectations of the capital markets; and a host of other players whose roles may not be obvious. These are the behaviors that so often seem to take you completely by surprise. The surprise is magnified by the speed of change in the increasingly real-time global business world: the people at the helm can't imagine how quickly and powerfully the winds can shift.

Internal realities include the organization's capabilities and behaviors. People often miss the external realities because they're overly focused on internal processes, policies, and politics. And yet that doesn't keep them from misjudging the internal realities. They overestimate their capabilities and underestimate the difficulty of achieving their goals. They believe people in the organization are behaving one way when, in fact, many are behaving quite differently.

From our experience and observations, we have identified six behaviors as the most common causes of failure to confront reality: filtered information, selective hearing, wishful thinking, fear, emotional overinvestment, and unrealistic expectations of capital markets.

Filtered Information. For all the information that's exchanged in business, it's surprising how often people miss the critical facts that could make all the difference. They may be getting information only from people with the same point of view. This is typically the case in organizations looking at the world from the inside out, rather than from the outside in. Or the information may be distorted by people governed by their own biases and pursuing their own agendas. In either case, leaders aren't getting reality from the source, from the people deeply involved where the action is. Instead, it is filtered through several layers of management.

Selective Hearing. The information may be good, but it's no good if the decision maker turns deaf when it's presented. Leaders practice selective hearing for a variety of reasons. The most common are preconceived notions or past experiences—looking into the rearview mirror, the arrogance of success—and the refusal to confront a problem because they can't see a solution.

Wishful Thinking. Wishful thinking is the root of much selective hearing and seeing. The acquisition will work because we need it to work. Sales will grow because we've promised they will. Any information to the contrary doesn't make it through the screen.

The urge to see things as you'd like them to be often takes the form of rhetorical statements supposedly based on experience. How often have you heard these kinds of sentiments:

"The market will come back—it always does."

"We've got the best people in the business and they'll deal with it."

"This has always worked, and it will work now if we just redouble our efforts."

At the extreme, wishful thinking is the hubris of overweening ambition, as in: "We will be the biggest player in this game within five years because I've staked my reputation on it."

Fear. Fear may be embarrassment over possibly saying the wrong thing at a meeting, or it may be a necessity in a culture of fear, where bosses punish people whose views are uncongenial. In either case, fear suppresses a lot of realism in the business world. Perhaps you saw this *New Yorker* cartoon: A stern senior executive is sitting behind a desk, a cringing junior executive standing in front. "Now," says the senior executive, "I want your candid, straightforward, and possibly career-ending opinion on this matter." No joke: We know of some tyrants who fired people for disagreeing with them. More common—and more pernicious—in companies that force-rank their executives, and where "attitude" is one of the criteria, people who make their superiors uncomfortable risk being downgraded to a lower performance percentile.

Emotional Overinvestment. People can accomplish great things when they're deeply committed. The downside is that their emotional investment in a project may blind them to its weaknesses. Often the mindset of the organization cannot accept a new reality because it goes against all belief and culture. Some of the most poignant victims of emotional overinvestment are companies with great histories of innovation. Circumstances change, substitutes come along, and nobody has the courage to say that the splendid history is just that–history.

Unrealistic Expectations of Capital Markets. It's vital to create value for shareholders, and business finally got the message during the nineties. The downside: many business leaders became captive to unrealistic performance expectations, notably the pressure for steady, predictable quarterly improvements. They responded by making unrealistic promises, which they often could keep only by bending their businesses totally out of shape.

■ ■ ■

EVEN PEOPLE WHO'VE BEEN REALISTIC during long and successful careers can succumb to unreality. Nothing is more poignant than the case of the leader who has executed a splendid turnaround of a business–facing its realities where others failed, and taking the courageous steps needed for change–but cannot confront reality when the situation changes again. Put yourself in such a person's place. It's been two years since they gave you this basket case, one of those situations that could make or break a career. You stepped in, did your homework, and developed a solid action plan. You reorganized, cut costs, installed new processes, and developed new products. You asked your people to make huge sacrifices, and they did. It has all paid off: your market share is growing, the business is making money, morale is high, the future is bright, and you're basking in well-deserved praise for your success.

Now comes a distant warning on the horizon: a competitor has started sourcing abroad, or the market growth you'd counted on for the next several years is drying up for unforeseen reasons. Sooner or later, things will turn sour. Having created something better than what you found, you now face the prospect of admitting that all your work was for naught. You have to tell your CEO or your shareholders that the projections you made are looking shaky or worse. You have to tell your people there's more bad news to come, more sacrifice ahead. In the worst-case scenario, you might have to say there's no solution at all in sight.

That's the sort of test that pushes normal human beings to their limits or beyond. It's not hard to understand why even highly intelligent and successful executives fail it.

NO MORE EXCUSES, PLEASE

Avoiding reality is a basic and ubiquitous human tendency. In some places, such as in tyrannical societies, it's a necessity. In open societies, it's a choice people make. Most people expect and even accept unreality in broad areas of public life, such as movies, television, and government policymaking. Many succumb to it in their private lives to keep peace in a family or a community. They often do it unconsciously but also may do it knowingly: sometimes, it seems, there's just no choice.

But businesses *do* have the choice to be realistic or not. Leaders of any business, from the largest to the smallest, have all the power they need to create organizations that can confront reality. And because they have the power, they have the obligation to use it.

Exercising the power of realism requires an open and inquisitive mind, intense curiosity, the intellectual ability to sort out complexity, the ability to persuade others, and—undergirding it all—the courage of inner strength. People who lack these qualities can't be considered leaders. They should look for other work.

Since business realism begins with a clear view of the external environment, the next chapter presents the big picture. It describes the structural changes sweeping the business world, and explains how they eventually touch practically every business in just about every place.

CHAPTER 2

Upended

Why the World Is Changing

As a practical matter, virtually every business is now a player on the global stage. But it's still hard for most people to see the specific ways global forces affect their businesses. People tend to look at them in piecemeal or linear fashion, failing to see emerging patterns. What they see often looks bewildering: a chaos of volatile exchange rates, competitive dynamics that are hard to define and understand, and uncertainty about a host of other complexities. The result is that more and more business leaders are getting blindsided, with a speed that was almost unthinkable in the past.

John P., whose story introduced the first chapter, is typical. He took all the usual steps to understand and deal with a new competitive threat, but they weren't enough. "Well," you may say, "that's life in the manufacturing sector: Go to China. Old story." Then how about Linus Torvalds? The Linux operating system he designed as a college student in 1991 and posted online interested only geeks at first. But over the years the free open-source software attracted more and more followers and developers. Now it's beginning to look like a genuine competitor to Microsoft's Windows. In 2003 Linux's share of the server market hit 24 percent; big users include Amazon.com and Sabre. Its share of the PC market rose to 3.2 percent, passing that of Apple's Macintosh software, and the growth seems certain to increase. IBM, Hewlett-Packard, Sun, and Novell are focusing on likely desktop customers in specialized operations, such as stock traders, engineers, and warehouse employees. IBM CEO Samuel J. Palmisano wants his employees to adopt Linux. Governments are interested, among them China and Israel; both plan to switch to Linux. If Linux captures 10 percent of the desktop market, analysts say, it will start to erode Microsoft's dominance in this market.[1]

The new rule is that almost any business activity is ever more likely to have a worldwide dimension. A new competitor can come from anywhere. The next Linus Torvalds—perhaps the one who could make life hard for your own business—may even now be developing his or her plans sitting at home in Bangalore, Shanghai, or Prague. It doesn't matter if this person is operating on a shoestring: a good idea is increasingly likely to find financial backers. And once any new product or service hits the market, it can reach customers anywhere on the planet almost overnight.

The other side of the coin, of course, is that the new global game offers unparalleled opportunities for those savvy enough to find them. If you're the first to see a market opening or the implications of a shift in regulatory policies, *you* could be the new competitor who blindsides a complacent player.

What's the reason for all of this, and will it continue? Understanding how the world business environment affects you starts with distinguishing between cyclical and structural change. Cyclical changes are part of business life's normal ups and downs, and any competent executive can deal with them. Structural changes are fundamental, long-term alterations in the basics of making money. They are usually hard to differentiate from cyclical changes in their early stages—which is when you really need to see them. By the time they're obvious, your odds of adjusting well to them are sharply lower.

Three structural changes are driving today's explosion of intensifying worldwide competition. One is the increasing integration of business activity across borders, accelerated by the Internet with its instant communications and vast repository of ideas and dialogues. Its most tangible aspect is the rapid growth of supply chains that stretch from the United States and Europe to all parts of the world—not only for goods, but now for services as well. The second structural change is worldwide overinvestment, fueled by a vast credit expansion and immense free flow of risk capital. The third is a global buyer's market that has shifted power from the owners and managers of capital to consumers and giant retailers. There's also a wild card. Around the world government regulators are getting more aggressive and they are coming at different issues, in different times and places, without coordination or rationalization of their policies.

ONE WORLD OF BUSINESS

The debate over economic globalism has traditionally been in terms of free trade, the exchange of goods between countries. As trade has become freer, though, something else has come along: a much broader dissolution of boundaries. Business leaders who worked in government councils to promote free trade, for example, envisioned more access to other markets. They recognized also that the flows would be two ways. What they didn't foresee was that they would someday be creating something bigger and more boundary-less than trade.

Japan's export surge of the seventies and eighties was the product of a finely tuned industrial machine in several key sectors of the economy, and it shocked American and European businesses out of an insular slumber. While some industries never recovered from the onslaught, many others took the opportunity to learn and improve. Today's global competition is another matter entirely. For one thing, businesses in developed countries have little to learn from upstarts such as China, Indonesia, Pakistan, Latin America, or eastern Europe. In fact, they are the ones bringing the knowledge. American, Japanese, and European companies are actively teaching managerial expertise and technical skills to the Chinese and others. The United States still has the world's highest productivity, and its growth continues to astound. The difference is in labor costs that are a small fraction of those in the developed economies, taking into account lower wages, lower benefit costs, and flexibility in work rules.

Even some still-developing economies are feeling the heat. Mexico, for example, is losing jobs to China and India. India is beginning to lose jobs to China. Cambodia worries that a good part of its textile business will go to China once U.S. import quotas that favor it are removed.

It's often argued that currency disparities are a major cause of these dislocations. Economic necessity will probably compel China to revaluate its yuan at some point, but it's not likely that will make much difference. China displaced Japan in 2002 as the biggest exporter to the United States. Foreign direct investment in China has been running at an annual rate of around $50 billion in recent years. A substantial amount of China's exports come from plants financed by companies in the United States, Japan, and other developed countries, and are integrated into global supply chains. A stronger yuan would not be likely to cause these companies to abandon the investments and related organizational infrastructure anytime soon.

This is one part of the structural rearrangement of global trade. The other part has even bigger implications for business, because it encompasses service elements that used to play only a minor role in trade.

In classical economic theory, countries enjoy comparative advantage because they have an edge in one or more of the factors of production, such as natural resources, labor, financial capital, and intellectual or social capital. But when the most important factors of production are fungible, old ideas about comparative advantage go out the window.

The factors that matter most today are knowledge and capital, and they know no barriers. The information age has produced not a global village but the global equivalent of a city or region. Just as supply chains stretch across oceans, capital, ideas, and new technologies flow around the world almost as freely and quickly as they would in, say, New York, Atlanta, or Silicon Valley.

On the demand side, television and the Internet have shown people in the so-called underdeveloped and developing countries what life is like in the developed countries. Most of them want to join the club—and for the first time in history, they have the opportunity to do it. They're willing to work hard, for not very much money. They have access to capital they've never had before. And they have access to know-how. All sorts of information is out there for the taking, from market data to the latest management techniques. Some of their information is expertise provided by businesses from the developed countries that train people to run their own low-cost supply bases.

Instant global communications networks allow these countries to produce not only manufactured goods but also all sorts of services essential to running a business, from the back-office and support staff to the product developers and even the R&D labs. Debates over job outsourcing have grown rapidly since the subject became a public issue early in 2003. As with many economic issues, experts are deeply divided over the long-term impact. As a practical matter, the outsourcing and insourcing of jobs will continue as companies seek to be competitive on a worldwide basis. And we'd argue that it shouldn't be stopped. There will surely be pain in the short run—no one can predict how much pain—but in the long run, the benefits will accrue to all nations.

A WORLD AWASH IN CREDIT AND RISK CAPITAL

A lot of what's making life difficult today is the aftermath of a two-decade investment boom. In the United States, for example, investment accounted for a third of GDP growth during the height of the boom, double its normal level of about one-sixth.[2] Easy money fueled the boom as borrowers took advantage of low interest rates. Private-sector debt rose to nearly 180 percent of disposable personal income during the 1990s—up from about 140 percent early in the decade and

100 percent during the 1960s. The result was "the biggest credit boom in its financial history."[3] Rising stock prices created more wealth between 1990 and 1997 with the market value of corporate equities rising from $3.5 trillion to $19 trillion.[4] And soaring productivity fanned the flames by lifting expectations for growth and profits.

As we know now, this was an overinvestment boom—what Morgan Stanley's chief economist Stephen S. Roach calls a "multi-bubble syndrome," from the Japanese bubble of the late eighties to the technology-driven United States equity bubble of the late nineties.[5]

In business, bubbles make for irrational investments and a lower return on capital. On the consumer side, they create artificial wealth through the inflation of assets. The bursting of these bubbles wrecked most growth strategies, ravaged returns on capital, left great amounts of excess capacity in many industries, and drove businesses of all sorts to clamp down on costs. Economies normally recover from such overindulgence by wringing out the excess capacity, adjusting expectations, and waiting for demand to catch up. That's starting to happen today in some industries and areas, but excess will remain a problem for a long time to come.

The whole world is awash in more capital than ever before. To a greater extent than any other sector, finance has become boundaryless—and increasingly unconstrained. Over the half century or so leading up to the nineties, the expansion of credit was controlled by a closely regulated banking system. Today it's more or less a free-for-all. In the old system, each country was a closed economy. Today there's no such thing. The global electronic financial infrastructure moves the capital anywhere, anytime, at the speed of light. As Nobel laureate economist Robert Mundell puts it, "The world is a closed system!"[6]

The new environment also creates credit on an unprecedented scale using sophisticated financial innovations–derivatives, secondary loans, collateralized debt obligations, and the like. Banks are no longer primarily arbitragers of risk but have increasingly become distribution channels for it. Lenders package and sell much of their credit exposure to unregulated capital market players such as investment funds, insurance companies, industrial companies, and private investors.

Debates rage over whether or not these practices could at some point destabilize the financial system. But there's no argument about the immediate impact. Credit in this global closed system is not only relatively cheap; derivatives make a growing proportion of it relatively low in risk for direct lenders. Based on estimates by the British Banker's Association, the global derivatives market could be worth some $4.8 trillion in 2004.[7] Because the primary lenders can resell their loans, they might not have the same incentive to examine risks as carefully as they used to. It's undoubtedly easier to lend money for a marginal venture if you're insulated from the consequences of its failure.

In the boom years, businesses invested against the backdrop of high expectations for revenue and profit growth. And as the *Economist* pointed out, "Cheap credit and inflated profit expectations cause both overinvestment and 'malinvestment' in the wrong kind of capital."[8]

The "malinvestment" ranged from the tens of billions squandered on fanciful dot.com ventures to more mundane expansions of unneeded capacity in industries of all kinds—(such as fiber-optic cables for telecommunications). Today excess capacity appears in all kinds of markets where existing and new players think they can gain advantage.

CAPACITY THAT WON'T GO AWAY

If the developing world is adding new, lower-cost productive capacity, you'd think that businesses elsewhere would get rid of their obsolete capacity. That's the way it's supposed to work in theory, and in the long run that may well happen. But much of this excess capacity has been around for years, in industries such as automobiles, commodity chemicals, and airlines. And more and more industries are suffering from it, from personal computers and software to telecommunications equipment. Barriers to entry are easy, because there's still a superabundance of capital looking for work. And barriers to exit are hard for several reasons.

It's a natural human tendency to not give up without a fight. Many players calculate that they have too much to lose if they unload big investments in physical and organizational assets at pennies on the dollar. Others hang in because each competitor has persuaded himself that he can be the last man standing. In the meantime, all of them fight viciously for market share to enhance their odds of being the survivor. Competitors will even *add* capacity, hoping that because theirs is newer and more efficient they can gain market share at the expense of others with older capacity.

The consumer electronics industry is a classic example. Highly efficient and innovative companies such as Sony and Panasonic drove American and European producers to the wall. Then along came more competitors, not only in Japan but in Korea and, most recently, China. Striving for market share and forgoing return on investment goals, every player drove prices down. Retailers and consumers have benefited tremendously, but hardly any manufacturer today earns the cost of its capital on a sustained basis.

Sometimes the players simply aren't being realistic. One way people fall into the trap is by thinking they have a specialty product when in fact it has become a commodity product.

For example, a business has succeeded for years by continuously improving its product through R&D. Along comes a new substitute for the product–not quite as good, but good enough for most of the business's customers. Nine times out of ten, the organization simply can't believe that its cherished baby, the result of so much hard work and innovation, has lost its place in the market. The innovators are sure they're making a difference, and indeed they are. The trouble is, they're not getting paid for it because the customers don't value the difference.

That's how AlliedSignal got a rug burn in the 1990s. Early in the decade, its nylon business was profitable and growing. Then carpet manufacturers, a big part of the business's customer base, were courted by domestic competitors that had developed a substantially less expensive fiber made from polypropylene. Allied's people looked at the polypropylene fiber and dismissed it as inferior. They went on with their incremental refinements for several years. Meanwhile the carpet makers were switching to polypropylene, and nylon sales dropped steadily. By the time people at AlliedSignal accepted what was happening, the business was losing money and had wasted millions of dollars improving a product with a declining market share.

Governments, too, play a role in maintaining excess capacity. In Europe, labor laws make it hard–sometimes almost impossible–for firms to shed workers. American companies have much more flexibility, but many are equally hamstrung by their "legacy costs," the pension and health benefits promised to employees that compel them to pre-serve businesses that would best be scrapped. Environmental regulations can keep unneeded capacity online. Oil, chemi-cal, and other heavy industries often can't afford to shut down obsolete plants because doing so would subject them to enormous cleanup costs. And government policies are sometimes deliberately designed to keep excess capacity afloat. Some big industries that employ lots of people, or are considered vital to national security, get various forms of help, ranging from subsidies to tariff protection and sub-rosa tolerance of cartel arrangements.

Then there's zombie economics. Who hasn't heard about the virtues of capitalism's "creative destruction"? Economist Joseph Schumpeter coined the term to describe the replace-ment of uncompetitive or obsolete businesses with fresh, vigorous new players. But a strange thing has happened over the past decade or so: companies such as US Airways, Uni-ted Airlines, Kmart, and MCI, which should be dead, man-age to walk around on life-support systems. They may go bankrupt, but they are rarely liquidated: there are plenty of lenders who will take their assets as collateral. Consolida-tions may shrink capacity, but rarely enough.

For example, most airlines can't make money on a sus-tained basis. Leave aside for the moment the high costs of unrealistic labor contracts. The big problem is the industry's excess capacity. True, some of the recent surplus has been cyclical, and some a hangover from the post-9/11 blight on travel. But the underlying cause is zombie economics. Airlines go bankrupt, but then they reorganize and continue to compete. Even in the rare cases when an airline is liquidated, the planes keep flying, thanks to leasing companies that own most of the airplanes. The leasing companies will do almost anything to get their investments into the air again—including offering cut-rate deals to upstart or reorganized carriers willing to fly them.

A BUYER'S MARKET: THE RISE OF THE KILLER INTERMEDIARIES

The business world has never before seen a buyer's market on the scale of this one. Barring global economic catastrophe, it's here to stay for the imaginable future.

It's no news that buyers call the shots when supply outstrips demand. And as anyone in business also knows, consumers are better informed, more skeptical, and more demanding. They can get information instantly on the Internet, and with more choices than ever, they are not going to buy your product if they see something more attractive.

What's unique to this era is the enormous help consumers are getting from retailers. It's ironic that as the Internet boom took off, one of the big buzzwords was "disintermediation." Electronic commerce, it was widely believed, would erode the importance of intermediaries because producers and end users would do more and more business directly with each other. While that has indeed happened in some cases, it has been overshadowed by a far more important development:

in major consumer market sectors, powerful intermediaries have created unprecedented distribution efficiencies. Ranging from huge retailers such as Wal-Mart, Home Depot, and Europe's Carrefour to Amazon.com and Internet auctioneers in the business-to-business space, they are making life extremely uncomfortable for some producers, while making others far more efficient.

The most powerful players in this shift are the so-called mass channel retailers. According to *Fortune* magazine, the ten biggest megachains in the United States account for some 80 percent of the average manufacturer's business, versus about 30 percent a decade ago.[9] Competing fiercely to win customers with lower prices and better value propositions, they are ruthless consumer advocates. The fewer customers a business sells to, the more power the customer has, so the big retailers increasingly control the profitability of companies and even industries that supply them.

A good place to see the power of the mass channel is in Bentonville, Arkansas, Wal-Mart's hometown, once a sleepy backwater. Between 1990 and 2003, the local population grew by 50 percent to more than 330,000 in the town and its surrounding metropolitan area, and researchers expect that number to double by 2025.[10] A substantial part of this population growth is due to the hundreds of Wal-Mart suppliers who have opened offices to oblige the company, which likes to have them close at hand. The offices typically display the maker's goods on shelves so that Wal-Mart buyers can see what they look like in the store. Procter & Gamble, Wal-Mart's largest supplier, has been in nearby Fayette since the 1980s; more have come more recently, ranging from Hallmark and Hershey to Levi Strauss.

■ ■ ■

YOU MIGHT THINK it a wonderful thing if Wal-Mart or Home Depot qualified your company as a supplier: just imagine the great volume of business you could look forward to. But you'd better be ready to meet a lot of tough demands.

A friend of ours learned the downside the hard way. John Trani is a superb executive, who transformed GE Medical Systems during the 1990s from a mediocre business into one of GE's stellar performers. When the troubled Stanley Works hired him as CEO in 1997, everybody who knew him looked for a repeat performance.

John succeeded at first. He restructured the company, halved the number of plants, and ramped up product development, which had been lackluster. He created a host of new market segments. Sales, profits, and stock price all rose briskly.

Unfortunately, the environment that Stanley and its traditional customers had enjoyed was changing, and those changes were about to accelerate. Before the mid-nineties, when the customers were primarily mom-and-pop hardware stores, consumers who wanted the best quality gladly paid a premium for Stanley's distinctive yellow label. The buyers were happy, the storekeepers got high margins, and so did Stanley. Prices rose each year.

As the so-called big boxes such as Wal-Mart and Lowe's became a greater part of the market, the situation changed dramatically. Several of Stanley's large customers went out of business because they were not big enough to compete with the big boxes or small enough to occupy niches. Among them were Hechinger's, Builder's Square, Payless, and a host of others. Selling to fewer customers is never good for profitability.

The shakeout also shifted the power at the negotiating table. The Wal-Marts and Home Depots don't have to make exceptions for powerful names. They can discount a brand's power significantly by giving a cheaper but respectable substitute the right price and placement and the promise–explicit or even implied–of comparable performance. In this environment, brands like Stanley are still valuable, but they're far from irreplaceable. No longer in the dominant position, Stanley and other branded players were forced for the first time to lower prices.

As a result, productivity gains became ever more important. Either suppliers would see their margins erode inexorably or they would have to find ways to offset the relentless price pressure being imposed. Mass channel players such as Home Depot were working at the time to compress margins, both for themselves and their suppliers. In the fight for market share, they needed to give their customers the lowest possible prices. (A colleague once heard a Home Depot director griping about the latest quarter's numbers. "Damn it, our margins went up!" he exclaimed. "Are you nuts?" asked his friend. "Oh no," he said. "We're not in business for that. We're going to make more money by putting more stuff through our stores and not by getting higher margins.")

Lowered margins were only part of the heartburn for Stanley. Home Depot also insisted on stellar delivery performance. This meant providing not only regular just-in-time deliveries but also large quantities of items on a moment's notice if they were needed.

Stanley confronted the reality of its new environment in several ways. U.S. production was clearly no longer economic for many product lines. For example, it cost 70 cents to produce a hinge in the United States versus between ten and twenty cents in China. The choice was simple: move production to China or wither. Stanley chose the former, and today its hardware business is thriving.

But the productivity gains and restructuring moves weren't enough. By 2001, sales to Home Depot accounted for more than 20 percent of Stanley's total, and more than 60 percent of some product lines. The company simply could not make decent money on those sales, so John shifted Stanley's portfolio to reduce its reliance on mass retailers. He sold off the residential entry door business, which depended heavily on Home Depot. Through new product development, distribution expansion, and a few large acquisitions, Stanley created its Security Solutions group, which sold and installed sliding glass doors and related hardware including locks directly to commercial customers.

The moves have reinvigorated Stanley's performance. It achieved record sales, income, and cash flow in the fourth quarter of 2003. In the first quarter of 2004, sales grew 20 percent and net income more than doubled. Analysts estimate that almost a quarter of Stanley's sales and more than a third of its earnings will come from Security Solutions by the end of 2004. Equally important, sales to Home Depot, while continuing to grow significantly in absolute terms, will shrink to 14 percent of Stanley's total in 2004. The dependency will likely fall further as Stanley makes more acquisitions that broaden its customer base.

John's accomplishments show that it's possible to survive and even flourish in a structural shift, but only with aggressive change and excellent execution. He recently told us: "Rationalizing production by moving to low-cost countries and reinvigorating product development were not enough to combat a very difficult industry environment. That environment will only get worse as the mass retailers gain share. Moving the business portfolio to more attractive markets and applying the rationalization skills our people learned have enabled them to continue to thrive."

■ ■ ■

STANLEY'S TROUBLES POINT OUT another trend that's making life harder for producers: established brands are losing their power. As *Fortune* magazine put it, "Retailers—once the lowly peddlers of brands that were made and marketed by big, important manufacturers—are now behaving like full-fledged marketers."[11]

Unit sales of store-brand goods have been growing at more than five times the rate of national brands. Wal-Mart's Ol' Roy dog food has passed Nestlé's Purina as the world's top-selling dog food, and the chain's George line of apparel has replaced Liz Claiborne in its stores. Close to half of the ceiling fans sold in the United States are Home Depot's own Hampton brand; an estimated 50 percent of products sold by Target are private brands; Kroger manufactures some 4,300 food and drink items in its own plants.

The pressure will only get worse for producers of traditional branded products. The fragmenting of mass media has weakened advertisers' power to connect with consumers.

The store brands can increasingly match or exceed the quality of established products. And retailers have huge incentives to keep developing their own brands. "Because overhead is low and marketing costs are nil, private-label products bring 10 percent higher margins, on average, than branded goods do. But more than that, a trusted store brand can differentiate a chain from its competitors. Shoppers will drive the extra mile to Costco to buy Kirkland cashews, filling their carts with other goods while they're at it."[12]

The consequences of the mass retailers' growing power cascade backward. Suppliers like Stanley pressure their own suppliers to drive costs down and compress margins, and they get rid of all but the most cooperative. (Just about every manufacturer we know has cut the number of its suppliers by more than 70 percent over the past decade.) And, of course, the major retailers are major drivers of the global search for lower cost production.

STRUCTURALLY DEFECTIVE INDUSTRIES

Many industries today are so crippled by structural change that their problems have no obvious solutions. We call them structurally defective industries. They range from such old-economy businesses as autos, commodity chemicals, and electric utilities to airlines, telecommunications, professional baseball and hockey, and the building materials industry, cut down by asbestos litigation.

Companies in these industries are chronically unable to earn enough to be economically successful, no matter how brilliant their strategies may be or how meticulously they execute. Their business models are broken and can't be fixed.

The reasons vary from industry to industry, but many are the result of globalization. They include excess capacity, crippling fixed labor and/or legacy costs, inept regulatory policies, and the behavior of competitors with unrealistically low criteria for returns.

Structurally defective industries limp along waiting for things to get better. Sometimes things do. Companies take people out and cut what costs they can; the business cycle heads up and they make a little money. They merge, hoping for greater market clout and operating efficiencies.

Nobody ever set out to be in a structurally defective industry, of course. And yet today these industries are purgatories for smart and talented people. Cutting costs and consolidating don't solve their fundamental problems: they merely create bigger struggling companies. The growth slows or evaporates, they're losing money again, and some are heading for bankruptcy (in many cases, not for the first time). Each peak is lower, each trough is deeper. Over time they don't earn enough to pay for the cost of their capital, which means they have no financially realistic reason to exist.

For example, GM, Ford, and Chrysler are finally seeing a payoff from years of hard work to bring their quality and productivity up to world standards. Their product and marketing strategies have improved. Though they can't yet match Toyota's ever-improving efficiency and cycle times, and are still burdened with numerous outmoded work rules that unions won in the past, they are generally competitive in the world auto market.

So why aren't they making the money they should? Over the past four decades Detroit's light-vehicle sales increased from about 8 million units in 1960 to nearly 18 million in

2000 before dropping back toward 16 million during the economic downturn. But operating margins have declined steadily, from a peak of almost 17 percent in 1963 to an average of less than 5 percent over the past decade.[13]

It's not just that the global auto industry suffers from overcapacity and feverish competition. Detroit's business models have been made obsolete by the huge legacy costs of pensions and health care for retired workers, and rising health-care costs for current workers. GM, for example, has 2.5 retirees for every worker. Its health-care liabilities passed $60 billion in 2004. Long-term pension liabilities are incalculable, but there's little doubt that they're sizable.

Competitors such as Toyota, Nissan, and Honda don't have comparable burdens, either at home or in their U.S. plants (where the workers are younger and mostly nonunion). Estimates of the cost differential per car range from $1,000 to $1,500—a difference no amount of improved operating efficiency, design skill, or operating prowess can bridge.

Detroit may be able to earn profits in good years, but unless the industry's business model is fixed, none of them are likely to earn the cost of their capital over time. There's no obvious solution, short of European-style government responsibility for health-care and pension systems.

REGULATORY REACH

As business becomes more integrated around the world, it's finding more and more of its activities in the crosshairs of regulatory bodies. GE, for example, would own Honeywell today had the matter been left entirely to U.S. antitrust authorities. But both companies do substantial amounts of business in Europe. The European Union's antitrust commission is a relatively new player on the global business stage, and it's an aggressive one. The commission didn't like the deal, and that was the end of it.

More recently, Brussels handed Microsoft a potentially significant setback. U.S. antitrust authorities hadn't been able to do much to crimp practices that are crucial to Microsoft's business model but that many people regard as monopolistic, including bundling such applications as Media Player with its Windows software. Early in 2004, the EU commission ordered Microsoft to offer computer makers versions without Media Player and also to share technical information about its server software with rivals. The decision could significantly affect Microsoft's software development and marketing strategy. Though the ruling applies only in Europe, it opens the door to challenges from competitors and governments around the world. If upheld, it also raises the likelihood of competition in an area that previously had been a virtual monopoly.

Expect the commission to intervene in more and more issues that a decade ago wouldn't have meant anything to businesses in other regions. As this book went to press, the EU's antitrust commission was also raising questions about Oracle's proposed acquisition of PeopleSoft. The EU has also become fixated on price fixing. Since the 1990s, it has been on "a cartel-busting crusade," according to *Wall Street Journal* columnist Holman W. Jenkins.[14] "Even the formerly tolerant British have declared war, including jail terms for miscreant executives and 'intrusive surveillance of suspect companies,'" he says. "Have enforcers uncovered an astonishing and novel epidemic of law breaking?" asks Jenkins. "Or has the crackdown merely pulled back the curtain on activities that are normal but seldom closely observed in the economy?"

He leaves no doubt as to the answer. The miscreants are more often than not "sad-sack commodity producers, often with high fixed costs, trying to divvy losses in times of slack demand." The supposed victims are giant companies like Coke, Pepsi, Procter & Gamble, Kellogg's, and Tyson Foods. "Strangely, though, these customers are seldom the ones blowing the whistle. Few of the 'victims' have even evinced any enthusiasm for a crackdown on their alleged tormentors, though some have felt obliged to file civil suits seeking damages once the prosecutions became headline news." Jenkins is not defending illegal practices, but rather pointing out that pricing in the real world is messier than it is in an economic textbook, and overall the prosecutions amount to regulatory overreach that doesn't serve any large public or private interest.

Regulators everywhere are also acting more often in the name of the consumer. In the United States, for example, federal agencies such as the Federal Communications Commission (FCC) historically set boundaries that protected players in industries from each other and outside competitors. Now the agencies ask: What benefits the consumer? The answer usually involves dismantling the old boundaries and opening markets to the greatest amount of competition possible. The results can create bewildering combinations of opportunity, risk, and damage, as the case of telecommunications in the United States shows.

CAUGHT IN A CROSSFIRE

Over the past decade the telecommunications industry has been hit by two external forces–technology and regulation– as well as the nineties bubble that resulted in massive over-investment.

The underlying environmental change began in the eighties with the breakup of regulated monopolies in the United States and Europe. But during the nineties, the combination of new technologies and government regulatory policies threw old competitive assumptions out the window, produced massive overinvestment, and generated chaotic levels of profitless competition.

Take just one part of the picture, the basic "wireline" business of the regional operating companies such as Verizon, SBC, and BellSouth. Wires–and more recently, fiber-optic cables–leading into homes and businesses are a multibillion-dollar infrastructure, and still the basic asset of the regional operating companies. But wireline revenues have fallen sharply in the past few years. The explosive growth of cell phone usage has been eroding wireline revenues at an accelerating rate, and cable companies are starting to woo customers away as well. Internet telephony, after a false start in the late nineties, is back in improved form and beginning to nibble at regional operating companies' revenues (along with those of long-distance carriers). Even electric utilities plan to provide telephony over their power lines.

Regulators, acting in the name of free markets and consumerism, have made matters worse. The goals are laudable, but the execution has been atrocious. Since 1996, regional operating companies have had to make their lines available to competitors offering local service. While the Federal Communications Commission set the policy, state regulators were left in charge of determining appropriate charges for the leased local lines. In many states, the regulators have set the rates with more of an eye toward consumer benefits than corporate health; no amount of cost cutting can counteract the revenue loss, and companies such as SBC argue that the wireline businesses now do not earn enough to cover the cost of their capital. A federal appeals court struck down the FCC policy in April 2004, but there's still no good ending in sight. Even if the ruling survives the inevitable appeals, it won't undo the damage already done.

Jockeying for the opportunities in the chaotic world of shifting regulation takes guts and nerve. Verizon CEO Ivan Seidenberg, for example, has said he plans to replace wires leading to the homes of residential customers with fiber-optic cable. His aim is to make sure Verizon can compete with cable companies in providing a full menu of high-speed information services. Initially, he announced a $2 billion, two-year plan to convert some three million homes. But if he were to follow through with Verizon's 32 million other customers, the total could reach an estimated $40 billion. Analyst Susan Kalla at Friedman Billings Ramsay calculates that it would take Verizon ten years to earn a payback of 12 percent on the investment—in an industry that historically has looked for a payback in less than four years.[15]

Is Seidenberg serious, or is he bluffing? It's not unlikely that the services he has in mind, from high-definition TV to interactive gaming, music, and even home security systems, could be provided at lower cost through copper lines with technically advanced DSL, or by wireless technologies now being developed. But Seidenberg is looking at a regulatory angle: the FCC has indicated that it won't force telephone companies to give access to competitors on fiber-optic lines to homes.[16] Given the uncertainty of regulatory policy, it's a breathtaking proposition even for the man whom *Fortune* magazine calls "telecom's consummate poker player."

But such is the nature of the game at the intersection of technology and regulation. The larger point is that regulatory reach is increasing around the world, and it can significantly affect your ability to make money. If it's something you haven't paid much attention to in the past, you'll need to spend more time observing it and understanding it in the future.

WHY DON'T COMPANIES SEE THESE THINGS COMING?

As we've noted earlier, leadership in this new business environment requires unprecedented awareness of a greater range of external realities than ever before. In the past the game has generally revolved around direct competition among similar players. Planners typically scan economic and industry growth projections when they analyze their opportunities and risks, but they put most of their time into studying the strengths and weaknesses of their most important rivals. Usually these are seen as traditional competitors in their home markets, and they are understood to have pretty much the same aims, such as profitable increases in market share and fatter margins. The planners look for ways to beat the competitors—build new low-cost capacity, develop a new technology, create a new marketing strategy, and so forth.

While the behavior of competitors will always be important, it is far too narrow a focus in today's business environment. Try looking at your own situation more broadly. You may have a great plan for beating the stuffing out of your biggest competitor. For example, you've got a promising new technology, and you're going to add some low-cost capacity to build the product. Nobody in the industry has anything like it. But how long will it be before a new player in China or India matches your product at a lower cost and places it in Wal-Mart? How good are your odds of earning back your investment with a decent profit?

Or say you can't get any pricing power right now. Is that really because the excess capacity you see is a cyclical issue, as your head of sales insists, or is the business already so overcrowded that nobody can make decent money in the long run?

What you intend to do to your competitor in your three-year planning cycle may not matter at all. More and more often, other players can set the direction the game is going in. Some are in your industry. Some are elsewhere in your value chain: suppliers and channel partners, for example. Some are in related industries. Some are completely off the usual radar screens, plotting your demise in small offices and factories half a world away. And some aren't in any industry at all—they are governments or players in the capital markets. Challenges to your business model, your strategies, and the very existence of your organization arise in improbable quarters. You are dealing today with something very close to the hypothetical butterfly of chaos theory, whose beating wings in China can ultimately generate a tornado in Iowa.

These winds can also bring enormous untapped opportunity. You can influence or even shape your industry. But you're not the only player who shapes it, and if other players can destroy its profitability, then you have to know about them and plan a different course of action.

So you have to understand not just the usual suspects, but also what can be called your extended industry, which includes all of the players who influence the industry's behaviors and economics. The behaviors of these players aren't necessarily the ones you take for granted. For example, like Wal-Mart, they may be trying to compress margins in their own and their suppliers' businesses in order to gain market share. Or like automakers in Korea or China, they may choose to add more capacity to an industry that's already awash in it.

This new reality requires you to do some soul searching and ask a lot of questions.

- Can you see growth in your industry?

- Is it profitable?

- Are supply and demand in balance?

- How far are the products of your industry from being commoditized?

- Are it structurally defective, or heading that way?

- How do you stand—realistically, without bias—in relation to your competitors? (We often hear people insist they're better than their competitors even when those competitors have higher margins and market share. Well, the margin and market share evidence suggest rather strongly that the competitors are better.)

- How do your products look through the eyes of the customer, especially the end user? Don't rely on internal assessments; the input has to come from the customer.

- Where is the technology going: can you foresee making breakthroughs with either one product or a series of products or a division?

- How does your talent compare with that of your competitor, and is it equal to what the customer needs? (Among the businesses we see, an alarmingly high percentage don't assess their talent as effectively as they should.)

- Do you have legacy costs that can sabotage your competitive advantage?

Where do you get the answers? Not from the planning staff, and not for the most part from your senior management team or your research director or the head of marketing. Unless they're extraordinary people indeed, they are like most others in the corporate world, caught up in the particulars of their specialties and their immediate business challenges, and looking at the world from the inside out. The solution is to take information gathering to the next level, which we'll discuss in Chapter 10, "Looking Around Corners."

THE NEW RULES OF ENGAGEMENT

Any assessment of the environment that begins and ends with "wait for things to return to normal" is long on wishful thinking. Global business integration, overinvestment, and the buyer's market redefine "normal" for companies of all sorts around the world.

Change can be friendly for people who embrace it. But in this environment, you'll have to be alert and move fast to capture the opportunities that change creates.

No matter what kind of business you run, from a multinational corporation to a corner convenience store, global structural changes have the power to take you by surprise. You may already be in a structurally defective industry and not know it. Even if you're not—even if you seem to be riding high at the moment—you could wake up wounded any day.

If you're a leader or manager in a big corporation you're most likely to worry about how to achieve global cost parity— the ability to produce at globally determined low costs. As the owner of a small business, you may need to look over your shoulder to see, for example, whether a mass channel player is coming to your neighborhood.

In either case, you can count on intensified competition. You probably already see it in your own industry or market, but that's not the worst part. More and more businesses are looking for opportunities wherever they can find them. With easy access to cash, players you never imagined as competitors, from other industries or areas, may well be eyeing your lunch even now.

This competition will mean shorter product life cycles and constant assaults on your differential advantage. The pace of innovation will continue, but the pace of imitation will increase at a faster rate. Ideas, technologies, and market feedback move at warp speed today, and businesses desperate for an edge seize them quickly for their own advantage. To beat them, you will have to *really* know your customers and end users with more depth and intensity than ever, and to speed up your own responses to their needs.

You may have to rethink your business model and determine whether it's time for a clean sheet of paper. Parts of your business that look good now can rapidly become less appealing in this environment, and new opportunities can arise just as swiftly. You'll have to be prepared to leave markets with limited growth prospects and move in other directions.

It boils down to this: we are entering a new era, defined by structural changes that won't reverse themselves anytime soon. Such epochal shifts have a habit of changing the rules for running a business, and this one is no exception. The next chapter explains why.

CHAPTER 3

Redefining the Basics of Management

Every age of structural change redefines management theory and practice. The post–World War II era, in which modern management theory took shape, was an epic seller's market, driven by pent-up demand and an explosion of a new middle class. Production people and accountants shared the driver's seat as managers focused on achieving ever-greater economies of scale through mass production. They ruled over a growing new breed of professional general managers–people who (so it was believed) could run any kind of business, and sell to anyone through ingenious new tools of marketing.

If one CEO can be said to exemplify the era, it would be the legendary Alfred P. Sloan, who made General Motors the world's largest and most powerful company. Sloan not only brought modern marketing to the automotive industry ("a car for every purse and purpose") but systematically and rigorously figured out how to organize a large business enterprise with diverse product lines and multiple customer segments. He pioneered the art of balancing decentralized operations with centralized financial controls, which became the model for many other companies, such as General Electric, as they got bigger. Sloan's innovations in organizational structure and processes can still be seen in large-business organizations across the globe.

From the late 1960s through the 1980s, acquisition and dealmaking became a major activity of corporate America. Especially during the grim seventies, with slow economic growth, soaring inflation, and interest rates that rose into the teens, there didn't seem to be much else to do. Merger mania began with a wave of companies called conglomerates—caricatures both of Sloan's model and the concept of the professional general manager. Most, like ITT, Litton Industries, Textron, and W. R. Grace, were assemblers of wildly diverse businesses; the idea was that cyclical ups and downs in the various industries would offset each other, providing a company as a whole with consistent, long-term growth in earnings per share.

If good professional managers could manage any type of business, why not? The great skill of top management was in crunching numbers and doing deals to yield the best financial results. Headquarters mainly contributed financial expertise; if a business delivered the numbers, it was left alone. If not, staff people were sent in to whip them into shape or replace them. Wall Street loved the idea of these conglomerates. It boosted their stock prices and price/earnings ratios; the higher valuations, in turn, helped them to acquire more and more companies.

The era's iconic CEO was Harold S. Geneen, the unrelenting number-cruncher who built ITT from a $750 million telecommunications company largely operating outside the United States into an $18 billion company with 250 profit centers, operating in more than twenty industries. But like conglomeration itself, ITT was a bad idea whose time came and went. Eventually it withered. Many businesses were sold off, and only a small portion of the original conglomerate remains today.

Through the 1980s it was back to basics. Acquisition took a new turn: corporate raiders such as Boone Pickens and Carl Icahn went after underperforming companies and installed executives who could straighten them out. "As a management fad they were never all that widespread, but they didn't have to be," noted *Fortune* magazine, "just as executing one mutineer can sober up a whole boatload of sailors, a few hostile takeovers left vast swaths of the American CEO class in mortal dread of their secretary's saying, 'Mr. Pickens on line one.' "[1]

Further sobriety was supplied by the invasion of Japanese manufacturers. They had been quietly building a manufacturing powerhouse by focusing on low cost, quality, productivity, and faster cycle time. Their operational expertise won them market share and high marks for customer satisfaction in some of America's and Europe's largest and most prominent industries, including autos, machine tools, and consumer electronics. It was the first time a global competitor had hit America's biggest companies in the belly.

The rise of Japanese companies and relative decline of U.S. and European stalwarts was every bit as controversial as the outsourcing of jobs is today. It provoked public fury and charges of unfair trade practices, people driving Japanese cars were excoriated as unpatriotic. But the popularity of Japanese products forced U.S. companies to face reality and hunker down. Business leaders learned to focus on operational excellence. They adopted new manufacturing processes, laid off unneeded workers, and slashed their

swollen middle-management bureaucracies. Concomi-
tantly, far-sighted leaders began to dismantle the traditional
command-and-control management model, pushing responsibility farther down in the ranks. Many built multinational organizations to compete in markets abroad.

GE's Jack Welch symbolized the age, transforming an
uninspiring diversified industrial giant into a tightly organized
growth machine and management model. Measured by its
market capitalization, GE during Welch's tenure became the
world's most valuable company.

The mid-nineties brought a boom of immense scale and
scope, fueled by technology, rising productivity, boundless
optimism, and unprecedented growth of risk capital driven
by an ever-expanding stock market. New laws governing retirement plans funneled huge amounts of middle-income
money into mutual funds for the first time. Also for the first
time, individual investors became a major force. The boom-
ing stock market meant that large funds could invest hundreds of millions of dollars in enterprises that ultimately
failed, often without significant effect on the investor. It also
meant that technology companies could attract talented
young knowledge workers by paying them with liberal
awards of stock options. Looser antitrust enforcement allowed industries to consolidate, turning the consolidators
into growth stocks. Eager for productivity gains, companies
spent heavily on computers and related new information
technologies: by 2000, IT spending accounted for about half
of U.S. companies' capital expenditures.[2]

Four mantras dominated management thinking during
the nineties: innovation in business practices, productivity,

speed, and creation of shareholder value. All were fine ideas, and they increased shareholder value and produced more wealth for more people than any previous era. But unintended consequences eventually undermined them.

Easy money drove both real and imaginary innovation, real in the sense of companies like Microsoft and eBay, imaginary in the sense of Enron and WorldCom. The obsessive pursuit of shareholder value distorted financial goals and compensation metrics of many companies. It also produced a generation of leaders who were essentially high-ranking financial public relations people, notable mostly for their skill at persuading Wall Street of their abilities to generate double-digit growth. And some new practices that arose because they ostensibly were in tune with the New Economy—such as valuing companies based on their revenues rather than on the money they make—proved to be fallacious.

Bill Gates is the iconic figure of the 1990s. Call him the father of speed: more than anyone else, Gates made the computer a tool for everyman, laying the foundation for the age of information technology. His unique business model helped to change the game from one dominated by a few players to a vast open market space that brought ever-expanding choices and ever-falling prices. (You'll find the details in Chapter 5.)

What Federal Reserve chairman Alan Greenspan called "irrational exuberance" came to an abrupt end when the stock market bubble burst. Now we are in a new era of structural change. It is at least as distinct and significant as the previous four. And more than any of them, it demands fundamental changes in the way leaders run their businesses.

To take just one example, it's almost impossible to over-state the magnitude of the changes being wrought by information technology. IT's impact may seem abstract when, say, you read about its contribution to productivity growth. It gets real when you look at a room full of people with laptops, and later see one of them sitting in a Starbucks connected to the flow of business by Wi-Fi. The point is not just that she's working harder and longer than ever but that she could be communicating with someone in India, China, or the Czech Republic. That's unprecedented. When ideas are instantly communicated and plans instantly executed through software that lets people collaborate across oceans, worldwide business integration can only become tighter and more widespread. Change can only become more rapid, competition more intense, and time to market more critical.

PHARMA AT A CROSSROADS

Past success has never guaranteed future success: it's an old adage, and never more true than now. Too much can change too quickly. Even powerful and successful businesses—or whole industries—can be battered or swamped by the storms of change.

What industry would seem to have a brighter future than pharmaceuticals, given aging populations and the growing body of knowledge about the human body? But today the pharmaceutical industry is at a critical crossroads as a result of worldwide competition, new technology, and spiraling health-care costs that have generated public anger over drug prices and portend increasing government involvement in the industry's future.

For more than two decades, pharma was a dynamic moneymaking machine without peer. Between 1980 and 2000, worldwide sales rose from $22 billion to $149 billion.[3] With estimated operating income typically in the 20 percent neighborhood, profits soared. During the nineties, the market caps of the ten biggest companies expanded by $1 trillion. Everyone loved pharma—investors for the double-digit returns, the public for the stream of blockbuster drugs that made people's lives better and longer, not to mention the professionals and managers who worked in the industry.

The industry's business model was that of a highly differentiated, high-margin producer. Years of intensive research produced such drugs as Warner-Lambert's Lipitor, Pfizer's Viagra, and Merck's Vioxx, and the high profits from those monster successes in turn drove more research. In many ways pharma resembled the movie business, with enormous up-front development expenses, numerous failures, and the occasional big hit that carried everything.

Margins in the industry are still lush by anybody's standards, but they are under assault from almost every quarter. Several factors have conspired to change the landscape. For one, product life cycles are shorter. In the boom years, drugmakers could count on long periods of patent protection—well beyond the decades-long expiration dates—by stretching and extending the patents with small differentiations. But regulators have become far more willing to open the doors to competition sooner, from both generics and so-called branded generics that deliver similar pharmaceutical properties with minor variations that skirt the patents.

At the same time, more and more drugs under development fail to make it to the marketplace. One reason is that the industry has already hit the easy targets. The big research challenges that remain, such as diabetes, depression, and various forms of cancer, are more complex.

The new competitive intensity has raised marketing expenses and has begun to compress margins. It has also led some drug companies to push the envelope in their marketing practices. State attorneys general, for example, have charged numerous drugmakers with billing governments at higher prices than the ones they charge doctors. And, of course, the price of drugs has become an immense political issue. The old pricing model depends on a tiered system, with the highest prices paid by U.S. consumers and lower prices paid elsewhere by public health systems that bargain prices down. The model worked well when relatively affluent Americans were willing to pay the higher prices. But with medical costs rising sharply across the board, Americans have lost their tolerance for the system. Imports of less expensive drugs, mainly from Canada, are now estimated to account for up to 2 percent of the U.S. market. Despite efforts to slow these imports, they are certain to keep growing.

The industry has tried to strengthen itself with mergers and cost cutting, and by reshaping its research organizations. While consolidation has helped a few companies, larger scale by itself doesn't confront the structural issues facing pharma. The moneymaking potential from licensed drugs, partnerships, and over-the-counter markets is a far cry from the lavish profit streams of the blockbuster era.

Unlike such structurally defective industries as airlines or commodity chemicals, the drug industry still has a world of opportunity. Aging populations and advances in science should guarantee both growing demand and supply. Most experts think the future lies increasingly in drugs produced through genomics, or targeted to an individual's DNA. But finding the right compounds is an immense and costly task. And gene-based drugs are typically aimed at highly specific conditions, for which the market is measured not in millions of people but in tens of thousands with particular genetic flaws.

Pharma's next era will almost certainly look different from its past one, with lower growth and lower margins, requiring changes in product development, cost structure, and marketing. In fact, what the pharmaceutical industry needs is a new business model. As we will show in the next chapter, only with an integrated analysis of their external environment, their financial target, and their internal activities can this (or any) industry successfully chart a new course and realize the substantial opportunities that remain.

A RETURN TO FUNDAMENTALS

The previous eras brought countless innovations in the theory and practice of running businesses. Many are now staples of contemporary management, but others were ephemeral distractions that led companies down the wrong roads. Too often, leaders have sought the appearance of success rather than its reality—size for the sake of size, bookkeeping profits as opposed to intrinsic value, earnings growth manipulated to please the stock markets. This era's changes are already redefining management theory and practice. Rising competitive intensity forces a return to basics again—but in a far more fundamental way than the operationally focused 1980s.

Getting down to basics today means first and foremost focusing on how you can create intrinsic or fundamental value for your business. During the 1990s especially, people equated value creation with a rising stock price. But fundamental value is a combination of real profit, real return on investment, appropriate cash generation, and growth that is sustainable based on continuing differentiation of your products in the marketplace. Your ability to create fundamental value rests on how good you are at finding the right balance between your external and internal realities and your financial aspirations: in other words, how skillfully you develop and use your business model.

A major reason to focus on fundamentals is that growth won't come easily. Organic growth will not often produce the double-digit gains that were routine and even obligatory in the last era. For many businesses, the battle to hold or increase shares of fiercely contested and slow-growing markets will be one of the three-yards-and-a-cloud-of-dust variety, won by fractions of points in market share and profit margins, and fought at every level from the top of the organization to the bottom.

Others will find brighter growth opportunities, but only if they're aggressive about finding new ways to do things. IBM CEO Samuel J. Palmisano puts it bluntly: "Either you innovate or you're in commodity hell."[4] If you plan to avoid commodity hell, you will have to be exceptionally alert to changes in your business environment and able to move swiftly to exploit them.

Leaders who hope to grow their way to success through mergers and acquisitions had better think again. Acquisition often looks like a nice idea because it promises to increase economies of scale or yield efficiencies from synergy—or at least show the kind of revenue growth that looks like progress. Sometimes it does. And some players thrive by picking up battlefield casualties on the cheap and hammering them into shape. Among the notable ones are Berkshire Hathaway and privately held Koch Industries, number two on the Forbes list of biggest privately held companies with estimated revenues of $40 billion. Many people viewed General Electric's acquisition in the 1980s of troubled RCA as a misconceived diversification ploy. But after selling off RCA's consumer electronics and aerospace businesses, GE wound up with NBC for a song, turned it around, and went on to build it into a network powerhouse. NBC generates significant profits year in and year out, and with the addition of Vivendi Universal's entertainment assets, is likely to significantly help GE's future growth.

But study after study in recent years has shown that companies that grow mainly through acquisitions are less successful than those that earn most of their growth organically. All too many acquisitions are done for the wrong reasons, and these are the ones that mainly account for the statistics of failure. A great many are paint-by-numbers exercises, with the goal being revenue growth (and often, though it's never stated, expansion of the CEO's turf and ego). "This merger will be accretive to earnings," a CEO will say. What he means is that it will make the stock more attractive, at least for a year or two, by boosting earnings per share. But an acquisition driven by accounting often has no specific connection with economic reality. It may result in fundamental improvements in cash flow or return on investment—or it may not. When it doesn't, the benefits of the accretive earnings can soon evaporate.

When industries are facing consolidation, the urge to merge among smaller players is colored by equal measures of fear and excitement. Fear drives some to defensive mergers that they hope will protect them from being subsumed in a larger enterprise. Others get excited by the hope of stringing together enough acquisitions to emerge as survivors. In either case, as with accretive mergers, the economics of the deals are secondary to the short-term benefits management can perceive.

Companies sometimes acquire with the aim of squeezing out the excess capacity in their industries. They hope this will level the supply/demand balance and improve the dynamics of making money. In most cases, consolidation merely buys time. The failure of such strategies is most glaringly evident in such structurally defective industries as airlines, automobiles, and commodity chemicals. It's also plain in industries where, say, a player with a new business model has made the models of others obsolete—as Dell has in personal computers.

Consolidation cannot return an industry's dynamics to "normal" if the players' business models have been overtaken by structural change. When most or all of the players are operating with broken business models, consolidation merely combines bad businesses into a bigger bad business. Just look at the airline industry. Mergers have done nothing to solve the problem of the industry's broken business model, and may even have worsened the troubles by distracting management from the core issues they needed to address.

The only good reason for an acquisition is to enhance the fundamental value of an enterprise: in other words, it must complement and strengthen the business model.

Another old practice ready for the scrap heap is that nineties holdover, maximizing shareholder value in the short run. As the dot.com phenomenon made amply clear, market valuations aren't necessarily connected to the fundamental value of a company. And investors fixated on quarterly results did a lot of damage by distorting management behaviors and distracting people from the pursuit of long-term value creation.

A widespread quest for fundamental value may speed the changes in corporate governance set in motion after the excesses of the nineties. If leaders are chosen for their ability to take care of business, rather than their charisma and bluster, fewer of them will be interested in cutting corners and bending the rules. The pursuit of fundamentals just might even put a brake on the endlessly upward spiral of executive compensation that increasingly makes American business an easy target for critics of capitalism. At the very least it's likely to link compensation more closely to the creation of long-term value.

This era will also require a new breed of no-nonsense leader whom we call the complete businessperson. The personality traits that traditionally get people onto the fast track, such as presence and communication skills, forcefulness, and the ability to motivate, aren't enough. Confronting reality requires business savvy and an unquenchable thirst to know, including the willingness to seek out diverse viewpoints and unorthodox ideas.

Complete businesspeople can master the business model

as the basis of their thinking and acting. The next section explains what the business model is and how you can use it to create fundamental value in your business.

The business model is the foundation of building fundamental value. As its usefulness and importance become more widely understood, we believe it will become the distinguishing managerial practice of this new era.

part II

Confronting Reality with the Business Model

When my leadership team took over at AlliedSignal in 1991, the automotive components business unit was inefficient and barely profitable.* We changed the management of the group, sharpened operating techniques, improved plant locations, brought in new manufacturing technologies, and instituted processes to help improve quality. We believed we could make AlliedSignal the best performer in its industry. Sure enough, performance improved markedly, and profits rose for several years. The turbocharger unit, in particular, developed into an attractive business with a clear differential product advantage and good growth prospects.

But the braking systems and airbag businesses, which together accounted for almost $2 billion in our automotive business revenues, were still struggling. Nothing we could do seemed to help. Finally we decided to sell the troubled parts, keeping only turbochargers and some smaller operations that had more promise.

It was a tough call. You don't casually suggest to your board of directors that you want to sell off 8 to 10 percent of your company when that board, like most, is looking for

*This section in the first person is in the voice of coauthor Larry Bossidy.

more ways to grow. But looking ahead, my senior management could only foresee things getting worse. "If we don't sell this now," we told the board, "we're going to have to give it away in a few years." After hearing the facts, the board agreed.

Reflecting on this sobering experience, we asked ourselves why we hadn't seen the solution earlier, before investing time and money doing all the right things to the wrong business. Not only time and money were wasted. In trying to make the business work, we replaced people who were, in fact, good leaders, doing the jobs they were hired to do and doing them well.

What I had to conclude is that we hadn't been realistic about the unit's ability to make money consistently. Allied had focused on doing a better job than its competitors, and in large part had succeeded, but the obstacles were greater than we realized.

Allied and its competitors alike made products that were essentially high-level commodities. We sold mostly to a very small number of customers, the U.S. and European auto companies, who themselves were struggling because their costs were seriously out of line with those of their Japanese competitors. These customers were so relentless in demanding lower prices from Allied and other suppliers that we even considered omitting margin information from the automotive earnings releases. Every time one came out, our customers would use the information to demand more concessions from our salespeople. The basics of making money simply weren't there, so trying to fix the business was a futile undertaking.

If one of the business unit managers had stepped forward at any point to say, "This business can't be fixed, and here's why," I would have heard him or her out and probably made the decision to sell sooner. But the managers evidently didn't have any better picture of the business's underlying realities than I did.

When we began this book, we looked back at the Allied mistake with the benefit of almost a decade of experience and observation. We came to see that it exemplified a fundamental and widespread flaw in management practice. This flaw regularly leads to bad and often fatal decisions—and yet nobody to date has really come to grips with it. The flaw is the absence of a clear, integrated picture of your business reality, calculated at the very beginning of any effort to plan a business's course.

Planning typically begins with the presentation of a strategy. We've seen thousands of such presentations, many of them highly detailed, complex, and bolstered with masses of data. But we've rarely seen equally detailed analysis of the exterior environment, the realism of financial targets that are set given the nature of that environment, and the organization's ability to deliver on those targets. These three elements are not harmonized, and as a result the plans are not realistic. That's why they so often take businesses in the wrong direction.

What kind of process, we asked ourselves, *would* take a business in the right direction? It would have to be one that modeled the business as a whole: in other words, a business model. But it would have to be a very specific kind of model, one that rigorously analyzed each of the elements and the relationships among them, and then harmonized them. We couldn't find any existing model that met these criteria, so we designed our own. We spent hundreds of hours developing it, refining it, soliciting critiques from respected business leaders, and testing it against all that we've learned over the years and all the successes and failures we've observed and analyzed.

The result, we are convinced, is the most comprehensive and useful tool to date for setting the right targets and action plans for a business.

Whether you own a gas station in a town like Ridgefield, Connecticut, are the CEO of a Fortune 500 company, manage a division or department within a company, or are responsible for developing profitable new products, our business model should be your most indispensable business tool. It tells you what enhances or inhibits the overall performance of your business—whether you have the potential to grow, make an adequate profit, and generate the cash necessary to pay employees, rent office space, buy raw materials to make products, market and promote the business, pay dividends to shareholders, meet the corporate goals for your unit, or earn enough from your business to lead the life you'd like to. It brings clarity to the fundamental direction of your business, and enables you to draw a realistic map for success.

Chapter 4 explains the business model. Chapter 5 illustrates its use, showing the business model in action and analyzing several historical business events through the lens of the model.

The New Model for Confronting Reality

The idea of making an investment in and selling something of value to a customer, making a profit on it, and collecting cash for it is ancient, universal, and down to earth. The simplicity of this idea is the essence of the business model.

A small shop in an Indian village has a business model. An entrepreneur with his first business plan has one. So do huge businesses such as Wal-Mart and the individual businesses such as aerospace and industrial products of diversified corporations like Honeywell International. Outstanding leaders in any business understand their company's business model, even if they don't call it by that name. Sam Walton and Michael Dell had business models in their minds. While competitors tinkered with their strategies, Walton and Dell used their models to transform the economics and competitive behavior of their industries.

Yet few concepts have more varied interpretations and meanings. It sometimes seems akin to pornography as described by the late U.S. Supreme Court justice Potter Stewart: "I can't define it, but I know what it is when I see it." To many people, a business model is just a financial exercise. Indeed, the concept didn't really get its name until the PC-based spreadsheet came along. The spreadsheet made it possible to do detailed analysis of every element of a business plan, and to plot the effects of variations in each upon the whole.

Others think of a business model as a sort of story about what the business intends to accomplish. It's often used to describe a business's place in the value chain. On its website, for example, software maker Red Hat asks, "What is Red Hat's Business Model?" The answer, in part, is: "Our mission is simple: To extend our position as the most trusted Linux and open source provider to the enterprise. We intend to grow the market for Linux through a complete range of enterprise Red Hat Linux software, a powerful Internet management platform, and associated support and services." Such descriptions may do a good job of explaining what a company intends to do, but they are a very small part of the total definition of the business model.

The version of the business model we've developed is an organized, rigorous way of looking at the health and profitability of a business, now and in the future. It is a statement of your current reality and its *likely*–as opposed to hoped-for–future direction.

It is also an early warning system for real-world changes that pose threats or provide glimpses of opportunities. The business model helps you understand whether the ups and downs every business experiences are the result of cyclical change, such as demand imbalances resulting from strengthening or weakening of the economy, or something far more serious, such as structural changes that can have a permanent impact on the profitability of any business or an industry.

Finally, the model is a blueprint for taking action. By using it to test the actions you want to put in place, you gain a better understanding of what will and won't work.

HOW DOES A BUSINESS MODEL WORK?

The business model starts with a logical breakdown of the many elements that make up a business, from its markets to its income statement to its leadership development programs. These group into the model's three components. The first is the environment your business lives in. The second includes your financial targets. The third includes the activities of the business: strategy formulation, operating activities, selection deployment, and development of people, and organizational processes and structure. Iteration is the process of

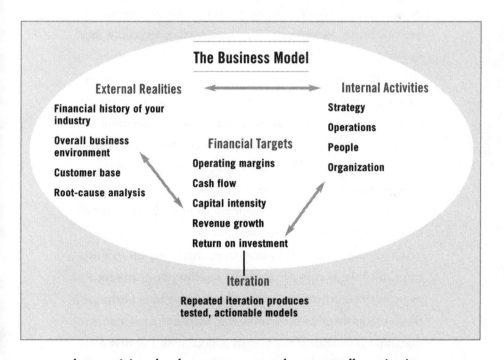

The Business Model

External Realities ⟷ **Internal Activities**

Financial history of your industry

Overall business environment

Customer base

Root-cause analysis

Financial Targets

Operating margins

Cash flow

Capital intensity

Revenue growth

Return on investment

Strategy

Operations

People

Organization

Iteration

Repeated iteration produces tested, actionable models

harmonizing the three components by repeatedly reviewing them as you add new information, and analyzing the subsequent changes in relationships among them.

Linking and iterating the financial targets, external realities, and internal activities, and searching for the right mix in each of the three components of the business model, is what determines the accuracy of the final prduct. These are demanding and challenging mental activities. It's crucial to keep four points in mind.

First, you must start with a general sense of the financial targets you want to achieve. They may be no more than aspirational, but they will be the benchmarks for analyzing the risks and opportunities you identify in the external environment, and assessing your organization's ability to act accordingly.

Second, the business model is not mechanistic. Some of its elements, like financial histories, are quantitative, but many are qualitative. Judgment is required at every step. You have to evaluate the qualitative factors—things like the nature and effects of trends, impacts of new regulations, distinctions between cyclical and structural changes, reasons why some industry players are more successful than others, and new factors that can affect your customer base for better or worse. You have to distinguish facts from assumptions. You have to test the assumptions you make against a variety of realities, including not only externalities but also the capabilities of your own organization.

Third, you have to be savvy in determining the relationships of all the components to one another. Realizing the full value of the business model requires looking rigorously at all three components, and identifying their linkages and relationships in developing decisions and executing action plans. This requires qualitative and quantitative judgments, pragmatism, intellectual honesty, confidence in information sources, and judgments about assumptions and risks.

Fourth, the business model is dynamic, not static. You'll almost certainly need several iterations—perhaps many—to get it right initially. After that you will need to test it regularly, keeping it up to date as you perceive external changes on the horizon and changes in own internal capabilities. But as long as you keep it anchored in reality, it will remain coherent through any alterations you have to make in any of its components.

ASSESSING THE EXTERNAL REALITIES

As noted above, every business needs an internally consistent set of financial targets. They are the backdrop through which you search for opportunities on the horizon and analyze current external realities. While your initial set of financial targets may be no more than aspirations at this point, they are benchmarks for comparison with what's going on in the outside world.

There are four elements of making a realistic assessment of your external reality:

- The broad business environment
- The financial history of your industry and its players
- Your customer base
- Root-cause analysis

The Broad Business Environment. Assessing the broad business environment means looking at existing and potential competitors; economic, demographic, and technological trends; regulatory issues; and structural and cyclical changes. This assessment is a rich mixture of quantitative analysis and subjective judgment. Searching both for threats and opportunities, you are examining the factors such as government regulations, technological advances, global influences, and new competitors, especially those that may come out of left field.

The global drive to lower costs (as described in Chapter 2) will continue to affect the business models of more and more companies. In the fall of 2003, for example, three supermarket chains—Albertson's, Kroger, and Safeway—entered a long and costly battle with their unionized workers in southern California over health-care costs. What caused the showdown? The answer is Wal-Mart, whose own lower health-care outlays in its rapidly expanding grocery business put the margins of the traditional supermarket chains under unbearable pressure.

Even in the wake of the settlement, it's not clear that the business models of the supermarket chains can survive in sustained competition against Wal-Mart, with its myriad operating efficiencies. Their chances today would be better if the companies had looked to their business models when Wal-Mart entered the game a decade before.

The Financial History of Your Industry and Its Players. At a time when whole industries are under assault, you need to calibrate the attractiveness of yours as an arena to play in. How has your industry as a whole performed in recent years, and how well have its individual players done? What are the growth rates, margins, cash flow, asset intensity, and returns to the owners or shareholders for as long a period as data are available? This kind of information is easier to get than it used to be, thanks to the Internet, analytical services such as Standard & Poor's and Value Line, and market research firms. But defining your industry may also require judgment about the industry's exact nature—that is, its segmentation and the dynamics of competition.

Your Customer Base. Your customer base is arguably your most precious asset. What could threaten it, what could broaden or deepen it, given industry and overall business environment trends and events? Trouble here usually comes from a loss of your differentiation, but what's the reason for it? For example, consumer electronics are marvels of innovation and technological sophistication. But their technologies are so fungible that differentiation is almost impossible to sustain except for a few powerful high-end brands.

Every business must sharply define the set of customers it sells to regularly and how that base will be retained, improved, or increased. Every business must also have an equally sharp and specific idea of why those customers prefer its products or services over the offerings of competitors: in other words, it must know them intimately. The quality of your analysis will depend a lot on how good you are at seeing your own business through the eyes of your customers.

Root-Cause Analysis. What are the underlying causes of the trends and issues you've identified? How is the money made, or not made, in your industry? Why do some players do better than others? For example, the airline industry as a whole is not a good business, but Southwest has made money over the long term and, more recently, JetBlue and AirTran have done so in the short term. Why? The pharmaceutical industry has a huge customer base and unique, innovative products that verge on being nondiscretionary purchases. Yet it's heading for more difficult times: Why? What do you need to know to judge the probable trend of your industry's profitability over the next several years?

Anticipating how your competitors and other players might change is another area of judgment: what has been is not always what will be. Supermarkets were not expecting competition from Wal-Mart; Dell surprised both Hewlett-Packard by selling servers and printers, and Best Buy by selling consumer electronics. The list goes on and on.

For businesses selling to other businesses, pricing difficulties may be due to a narrow customer base—usually, the fewer customers you have, the more advantage they have. It's also important to understand their business models: recall the lesson of AlliedSignal's automotive unit. Companies that do a really good job of providing solutions to their customers can sometimes help them with their own business models.

When you're doing your analysis, don't let your thinking get boxed in—that is, don't passively accept things as they are. Michael Dell and Sam Walton changed their industries, and made their competitors' business models obsolete. So did Rupert Murdoch. His acquisition in early 2004 of DirectTV completed his global satellite distribution system and created the most powerful combination of media content and distribution in the world. Some critics argue that the model is flawed, but no matter. Murdoch is forcing cable companies like Comcast and even telecommunications companies to fundamentally reexamine their options for making money in the years to come.

Because they had unique insights into the dynamics of their external environments, Dell, Walton, and Murdoch changed their industries. You too, whether you're a CEO, a division or department head, or an entrepreneur, could find ways to challenge your industry with a better business model.

THE FINANCIAL TARGETS

Every business needs an internally consistent set of financial targets. As you search back and forth to determine the right relationship between each component of the business model, you develop a basis for adjusting the targets to reality. The purpose of these targets is not to strive for precision over, say, a three-year period but rather to recognize that the changes you observe in the external environment, as well as most changes in internal activities, have consequences that must be recognized in the financials. Without the discipline of the model to guide them, most people do not connect the external realities with internal activities.

Companies often set their financial targets almost in a vacuum. In many cases their budgeting processes are numbers and gaming exercises, where people at lower levels focus on protecting their own interests rather than the realities the organization faces. Sometimes people are driven by the demands of others: financial markets, or the CEO, or the head of the division, dictate what the goals should be. Sometimes these are based on little more than the executive's hopes and dreams. A typical scenario—we've seen it many times—is that the CEO wants his company to rank with the top quartile for earnings-per-share growth in the S&P 500. That's well above the average for his industry, but no matter. He tells his team to develop a bold strategy that will get him there. He may be motivated by hubris or by an admirable (if misguided) can-do attitude; and he may or may not succeed. In either case, the point is that he's taking unnecessary risks, because he doesn't have a real-world basis for setting the goals.

The analysis of the external environment gives you a realistic context for setting the appropriate financial targets. Say a business unit leader's team is enthusiastic about a new idea for a strategy they believe can grow revenues at 8 percent a year. She knows that the industry's recent growth rate has been only 3 percent. In her root-cause analysis, she compares the strategy with the trends she sees in the business environment, along with her unit's operating and people capabilities. At the end, after seeking other points of view from people inside and outside the business, she realizes there's nothing in the mix that could produce the hoped-for outcome. The strategy will work only if the team can come up with a new and significantly better way to differentiate the unit's product.

Which are the most important targets in your business? Rarely will anyone be able to assume lofty goals for all of the targets—at least, not in the short run. You usually have to make trade-offs. For example, if you want higher margins, you will need to differentiate your product, most likely by spending more on technology or innovative marketing programs. If you want to finance expansion but are concerned about your capital structure—maybe you're already carrying a lot of debt—you will make cash flow a priority.

STRATEGIES, OPERATING ACTIVITIES, PEOPLE, AND ORGANIZATION

Only after you've crystallized the realities of the external environment and linked them with your chosen set of financial targets can you go on to think about strategies, operating activities, selection and development of people, and organizational processes and structure.

Operating activities include the programs and processes that enable your business to reach the desired financial targets and execute strategies, such as product launches, sales plans, and measures to improve productivity. Dell's famous supply chain is one of its critical operating activities; so is Southwest Airlines' ability to turn a plane around in roughly a third of the time its competitors need. People selection and development also includes deployment of people—are the right people in the right jobs? A major reason for the mismatches between goals and results in most businesses is the lack of connections between these components and the strategies: often each in its own silo, and their integration is a hit-or-miss affair.

Consider the typical planning process. Leaders draft a strategy to figure out how the business will be positioned and differentiated against the competition. People often rely on staff planners, and sometimes on consultants and investment bankers, to help design the strategy. They identify opportunities in the marketplace and come up with ideas about how to take advantage of them—by, say, leveraging scale to reduce costs; using technology to provide better products or services; or achieving growth by expanding geographically. They create a financial forecast to see what benefits the strategy might produce. Then they determine, based on the strategy, the operating activities and structure of the business.

Here's the problem: all the people involved in the planning process are doing their work outside of the business model. There's too much emphasis on getting the forecast first: "We've got a great strategy, and here's what we expect it can give us." The process doesn't develop the meticulous and comprehensive financial expression of the environment that is the foundation of realism. These forecasts typically *assume* that the business's managers will implement the operating activities, people deployment, and organizational processes needed to achieve the strategy's projected financial targets. And whatever time is spent on looking at the environment is usually devoted to the specifics of competitive dynamics within the industry. That's what happened, for example, with the AlliedSignal automotive business. As should be clear by now, that's too narrow a cut.

What's more, it's harder to stay intellectually honest in a strategy session. By the time a strategy's creators do the financial forecasts, they have invested a lot of intellectual and emotional energy in the strategy. They're preoccupied with its details, and they aren't in the mood to hear bad news. Unconsciously, at least, they tilt toward assumptions that support their hopes and dreams, and downplay those that don't. So the numbers will almost surely come out looking good. But the odds of actually making those numbers are not so great. It may require an uncommon amount of good luck—including the probability that your competitor's strategy process is no more realistic than yours.

Strategy assumes its rightful place in the hierarchy of decision making when it's part of the business model: integrated with the realities of the external environment, the financial targets, and the business's operating, people, and organizational activities. Wishful thinking and emotional investments don't drive the decisions. Through the business model all three are linked simultaneously and iterated back and forth until they match reality.

How do you think about strategy in the context of a business model? You start with a series of questions such as these:

- If your industry is delivering financially attractive results and you aren't, what are the reasons? How do these factors bear on your strategy, products, technology, distribution, operations, people, and organization?

- If the industry is underperforming, is there something you can do to overcome the root causes? At AlliedSignal automotive, for instance, the strategy of focusing on the turbocharger unit created a differentiated and solidly profitable business in a generally bleak environment.

- How can you develop plans that are flexible, which provide directions to go in rather than specifics? Many strategic plans are linked to fixed yearly projected numbers for three to five years. This kind of planning is very rigid. Numbers are not strategy, but the financial expression of what strategy will accomplish each year, based on assumptions about the market, competitive patterns, and your capabilities at the time. All of these can (and almost certainly will) change. Instead, you have to plan directionally: what mix of actions do you plan to take, and what's the range in which your resource allocation will take place? When one or more of the variables changes, you will have the flexibility to respond.

- What productivity initiatives, such as enterprise resource planning (ERP) systems or outsourcing, will make you more competitive by lowering your costs?

- Do you have the resources to finance the strategies and initiatives you've identified?

- How good are your operating activities? Do they ensure that your strategy provides distinctive experience to your customers, and deliver one or more financial targets?

- Do you have the right people to pull off the introduction of new initiatives? Are they properly deployed—are the right people in the job?

- What obstacles in your business stand in the way of reaching your goals? For example, why do competitors have better margins? Why does it take your organization longer to get new products to market?

- Are you focusing on the right initiatives for growth? To grow at a faster rate than your industry, you need some edge—a cost advantage that enables you to sell at a lower price, new and better distribution channels, serving parts of the world not yet served, a breakthrough technology, better knowledge of the customer, a more effective organization.

The business model gives you an understanding of the industry and all the factors in the broader environment that are likely to affect it, along with the capabilities of your organization to execute the strategy. This allows you to test the validity of strategies before wishful thinking and emotional investments gain momentum. In some cases multiple iterations of the business model do not yield results consistent with your aspirations. In these cases you either have to change your financial aspirations or revise your internal activities.

The fact is that most troubled businesses didn't decline overnight; the seeds were sown long before. At the beginning of the 1980s, for example, Kmart was prospering with a business model that had served it well for decades: the company undercut department store prices, making more money on smaller margins because it built and ran its stores with lower costs. But Wal-Mart was growing much faster. It was winning customers from Kmart even though it didn't have the same leverage in purchasing as its bigger competitor. This should have been a signal to Kmart's leadership that their business model was under pressure because Sam Walton was doing something different, and that they needed to understand what it was.

Walton got his start in towns and regions that weren't served by the big retail chains, which initially didn't pay much attention to what he was doing. But his business model was to underprice the discounters like Kmart, and it was expressed in his famous mission statement: "I will always lower prices." His margins were even lower than theirs; he made his money by managing for faster inventory turnover. He achieved that through another operating activity: closely scrutinizing customers' needs and responding immediately.

As Wal-Mart grew bigger, Walton developed a distinctive and powerful operating activity. He allowed his regional managers to use private planes so they could personally visit their stores and return each week to Bentonville to share information and plan deliveries to the stores of the right merchandise at the right time. Eventually he developed industry-leading precision systems that reached back into his supply chain to create flows of goods based on demand in real time.

Walton also distinguished his business with the type of people he selected and deployed. He looked mainly for hard-working junior-college graduates who were highly motivated to find their way in the business world—people who were not afraid to start at the bottom and work their way up, and who would be comfortable in small towns.

Walton's business model created a structural change in retailing, and during the nineties, it overwhelmed competitors such as Kmart. Wal-Mart's advantage widened as the company aggressively pushed suppliers to give it lower prices—and helped them to do so by teaching them how to improve their inventory turns and cut waste in the flow of goods from their factories to Wal-Mart's loading docks. Indeed, Wal-Mart had from the outset focused on the flow of goods as a critical operating activity, constantly updating Sam Walton's famed system to stay on top of customers' buying preferences, reduce inventories, and increase its own velocity. When you see trucks arriving at a Wal-Mart store like clockwork, each meeting its allotted time slot for delivery, you're seeing Walton's business model in action—it's literally where the rubber meets the road.

By the end of the decade, Wal-Mart's sales had passed those of Kmart, and they kept accelerating. Had Kmart's leaders studied the two business models carefully, they would have learned how Wal-Mart was pulling this trick off. Root-cause analysis would have unearthed Sam Walton's secret; it was there to be seen by sharp eyes. Wal-Mart enjoyed growing advantages, including higher sales per square foot of retail space, lower advertising costs per dollar of sales, and higher cash flow—which it used to help fund its rapid expansion. Store managers were empowered: they would interpret customer demand patterns, and the Wal-Mart system would respond immediately. And associates on the floor had the satisfaction of seeing pleased customers leave with the goods they wanted at prices that made them happy.

Yet Kmart's leaders still failed to see the significance of both Wal-Mart's pricing strategy and the operating activities that sustained it. Instead, they put their resources into positioning and pricing strategies—signing on Martha Stewart, for example, and at the same time cutting prices aggressively. Such measures, while helpful in generating sales, couldn't possibly get to the root of the problem of the obsolete business model. Kmart's cost disadvantage continued to grow, and its cash flow turned negative. Its supply chain was inefficient and its inventory systems were primitive, leaving it out of stock on many popular items and grossly overstocked on others. In the years before it went bankrupt, many stores looked like they belonged in the old Soviet Union, with shoppers wandering disconsolately through aisles with bare shelves on one side and piled boxes on the other. Kmart has made a lot of progress since then, but it is now a much smaller player in its industry.

ITERATING THE MODEL

As we noted earlier, the business model is dynamic—you must regularly revise it as circumstances change. Rarely if ever will your first cut provide all the right answers. Iteration is how you put different pieces into the mix and keep searching until you get the solutions that harmonize the model.

As you work through the external environment and your internal activities, your financial targets will change according to the realities you've identified. Each iteration deepens your understanding of what you can and cannot reasonably expect to accomplish. You identify areas where you may be able to improve your performance—or ones that you thought held the promise for improving it but which, under scrutiny, do not after all. You learn whether or not all the moving parts of the plan mesh with each other. Each of these discoveries is a new iteration of the business model.

The iteration process is where you make trade-offs. Too many plans try to be all things to all people. But the reality of business is that you can't always get what you want. Trade-offs are inevitable in planning and running a business. For example, achieving growth may require heavy investment or building market share through aggressive pricing, which will probably require you to adjust your financial targets to include lower earnings in the short run.

The final product may be for one year or several, depending on the length of your industry's cycle. In either case you'll iterate it again in the following year (or sooner in the case of unexpected and rapid changes in circumstances). And it can be used as a regular test of your ability to properly assess your business realistically. This is particularly important in multi-year plans, which are notoriously subject to unreality. For example, Joe has shown you a plan with the famous hockey-stick revenue curve—it shoots upward in the third and final year when everything comes together. But Joe expects that he'll have moved on to greater things before then, so he won't be around to take the heat if it doesn't work out that way. A properly constructed business model helps identify people with Joe's intentions.

Sometimes there's simply no good match to be found among the components. Even after multiple iterations there's no harmony: the model doesn't yield results consistent with your financial aspirations. What then? You either have to change your financial aspirations or revise your internal activities until they're consistent with each other.

Iteration is also where you apply and develop your business savvy. A business model by itself is no guarantee that you'll make all the right moves and succeed. Two business models can look exactly alike on a piece of paper but they can be dramatically different because of the quality of work that went into making them. It takes good judgment and intellectual honesty to bring these iterations to a realistic conclusion. It also takes emotional tenacity: you can't consider yourself done until you and your people have exhausted your thinking. These are the qualities that will determine the ultimate validity of your model.

CHAPTER 5

Getting to Reality

Before you start developing your own business model, it may be useful to see how others have managed the process. This chapter offers practical guidance in working with the business model and in using it to understand a changing business environment. The two examples that follow are stories that we know firsthand from working with the leaders.

UNRAVELING A MYSTERY

We talked in the fall of 2003 with the leader of a consumer goods business—we'll call him Richard—emerging from fifteen years as an also-ran in its industry. It had the best-known brand in its industry—one of the top twenty in the world—which was sold mainly by mass discounters like Wal-Mart. But it was making little money; cash flow after interest on debt was consistently negative, and market share was shrinking. Over ten years, three previous division heads tried to get the company out of its rut, each focusing on an operational tactic in which he had expertise. One was a marketing whiz who thought the answer lay in new-product introductions. Another had a background in advertising; not surprisingly, he changed advertising agencies and launched a new ad campaign. Another was a cost cutter, who closed plants and cut rather indiscriminately. As each change in operating activities failed to produce the hoped-for results, the leader was replaced, subjecting the division to tremendous turmoil and perpetuating the financial drain on the corporate parent.

Richard joined the division from another consumer goods business where he'd built the brand into a world leader. He set out to identify the realities of moneymaking in his new assignment using the business model as a tool—something nobody there had done before. It didn't take much digging to see that the financial situation was getting critical; Richard was likely to have trouble getting funding when he went to the bankers to refinance the division.

Was the brand simply on the skids? In analyzing the external realities, Richard talked to his customers, the ten largest of which accounted for some 80 percent of sales. Customers like Wal-Mart had made it clear that they felt the brand had value; they wanted it to survive.

Richard had to know how competitors were making money, what they were doing that was different. He asked his CFO to analyze the business models of two competitors who were gaining market share, but the CFO didn't understand operations; his main role had been as a link to the bankers. Frustrated, Richard hand-picked some people to gather the information and do an unbiased analysis.

When they were done, Richard finally understood the reality of his division's business model compared with those of his two major competitors. The table shows the salient details that emerged from the analysis.

COMPANY	RICHARD'S BUSINESS	COMPETITION A	COMPETITION B
Revenue	$1 billion	$1.3 billion	$1.2 billion
Gross margin	46%	70%	72%
Distribution cost	15%	16%	16%
Merchandising cost	14%	15%	15%
Media cost	12%	27%	30%
Net profit	5%	12%	11%
Price per unit	$10	$9.50	$9.50

One item leaped off the screen: the gross-margin comparison. "I was horrified," Richard told us, "the more so since our unit pricing was higher than our competitors'." As he tried to unravel the gross-margin mystery, he saw that costs, which are part of the gross-margin calculation, had a very different mix. The competitors spent much less on product mix, formulation, and packaging, and their higher gross margin allowed them to invest disproportionately more in media. As a result of higher and more extensive media spending, they were gaining shelf space, increasing revenue and market share, and building brand equity.

Richard's predecessor had missed the connection between media spending, shelf space, brand growth, and revenue growth. He had launched an across-the-board cost-cutting program, including cuts in media spending, without giving enough thought to how those cuts would affect other parts of the business model. This backfired in two ways. First, it clearly played a role in the loss of market share. Second, and not so obvious, it also hurt on the cost side. When you lose market share in a consumer goods business, retailers naturally want to reduce your shelf space. The division could preserve its shelf space only by giving the retailers higher discounts.

"It was clear that our product and operating costs were way out of line, and that we couldn't make a living this way," Richard said. The issues underlying the gross margin turned Richard's attention to internal activities, the third component of the business model, where he found a variety of operational problems, including production inefficiencies and high packaging and ingredient costs compared with industry norms. He also found a proliferation of SKUs (stock-keeping units as identified by retailers), mainly for small variations in size and packaging.

Reducing the product variations would be simple enough. But after reviewing his leadership team, he realized the other issues would require attention to the people element of the third component. He brought in executives who were creative with formulation and packaging. In short order, they cut costs significantly without compromising the qualities that mattered to customers.

He also brought in marketers who could think creatively. They winnowed out supernumerary products and came up with not another new ad campaign but a more effective way to spend on media. The previous marketers had focused mainly on national TV campaigns, and had pursued them erratically—spending less in some years and more in others, and switching themes frequently. The new approach was to reduce national TV advertising and concentrate resources on regional advertising, working jointly with Wal-Mart, and adding resources for print advertising and couponing.

When we talked with Richard, he had just come from a meeting with his bankers. Their faith in the company had waned over the years, and they were just about out of patience. But attitudes changed 180 degrees when he showed them the new analysis and actions derived from the business model, and explained why and how he could use his knowledge to gain profit leadership in the industry within two years. The meeting ended with their commitment to a major new financing that Richard would use to rejuvenate the company.

MODELING THE SOLUTION FOR RICHARD'S BUSINESS

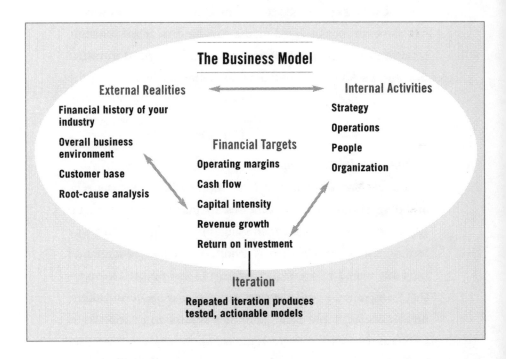

The Business Model

External Realities ←——————→ Internal Activities

Financial history of your industry

Overall business environment

Customer base

Root-cause analysis

Financial Targets

Operating margins

Cash flow

Capital intensity

Revenue growth

Return on investment

Strategy

Operations

People

Organization

Iteration

Repeated iteration produces tested, actionable models

External Realities: Competitors were gaining market share and making better profits. Yet consumers liked the brand and retail customers wanted it to survive.

Financial Targets: Gross margins were substantially lower than those of competitors, and cash flow was negative.

Internal Activities: Previous managements had tried to turn the situation around with new product introductions, shifting advertising campaigns, and across-the-board cost cutting, but to no avail.

Iteration: Root-cause analysis, including modeling of competitor behaviors, revealed the discrepancy between the components of Richard's margins and those of his competitors. Searching for specific measures that would allow him to raise his financial targets, he pinpointed lower formulation and packaging costs and reduced product variations as ways to raise cash for increased media spending. This led him to make people changes, bringing in executives with formulation and packing skills, and new marketing leadership.

THE POWER OF FACTS

In 2000, Michael Wisbrun was appointed head of KLM Air Cargo. He had worked for the division earlier in his career, and then in other KLM businesses. Its management team, a group of conceptual idea-men guided by a major consulting firm on a long-term basis, was trying to execute a vision that they felt would reinvent the industry. They rightly foresaw that companies would develop more and more worldwide networks and supply chains, and they wanted to position Air Cargo as a leader in the emerging trend.

Instead of merely shipping cargo from a KLM point of origination to a KLM destination, the division would provide customers with a seamless flow from loading dock to receiving dock, using sophisticated information systems and logistics expertise. Whether the customer wanted to ship pharmaceuticals or electronics, animals or flowers, KLM would oblige with integrated, point-to-point logistics and integrated supply chain delivery service between Europe, North America, Asia, and South America. The division had recruited people to shape the strategy in detail and had begun to make huge investments in IT and other logistical ingredients to put it into action.

But Wisbrun had serious reservations about the business model he inherited. When he looked into the second component, the financial targets, he saw that the division had flat revenues, and was barely breaking even. Cash flow was negative, and the return on investment was approaching zero: not a great foundation for a bold, unproven strategy.

Worse, his external analysis of the new model turned up a major flaw in the vision. Large integrators such as FedEx and UPS were already serving the market; not many customers were looking for similar service from an airline, and those that were didn't seem willing to pay for it. They might be in the future, but for now the structural change in the cargo transport market the planners imagined wasn't a reality.

Even if the market had been ready and willing, the internal operations and organization were a poor match for what the new approach required. The kind of operations the management envisioned would require a briskly service-oriented organization with precise coordination to manage the scheduling intricacies. But KLM Cargo had a fragmented organization structure, lacking in integration and accountability.

"The business model clearly wasn't anchored in reality; its

parts didn't mesh," says Wisbrun. Observing that some competitors were making money in their conventional air-freight businesses, he reasoned that KLM Cargo could too by strengthening its core business. The business model would be not only his guide, but also his ally in getting the organization aligned. "The power of facts is tremendous," he says. "And the simplicity of the business model creates a basis for the power of facts. People can see the need for change."

He established clear and specific financial targets—a critical element in confronting reality—and set them quarter by quarter for the next eight quarters. He then turned to the third component to see what changes would make it possible to meet the targets. The answer, he concluded, lay in getting the right kind of people, reshaping the organization, and developing stronger organizational processes.

Wisbrun shut down the ambitious logistics plans and huge IT investment, and created a new three-person management team of seasoned operating people, called "The Delta Team." He worked with them to determine the people and organization processes needed to drive the change. He replaced some of the bright conceptual people who weren't experienced in line jobs with ones skilled in operational execution—leaders who could do the intensive blocking and tackling needed to generate cash, margins, cost savings, and market share gains.

Managing for cash received intense focus. Accounts receivable were a mess, with unacceptable delays between billing and payment, and too many planes were flying only partly filled. Tightening accounts receivable procedures cut days outstanding in half, and coordinating shipments booked by the various business units improved asset utilization by 40 percent. Cash generation improved substantially.

As his plan moved forward, Wisbrun regularly coached his management team using the tool of the business model. Every six weeks, for example, they would drill down into the financial targets to see if the relationships among them held together and the targets were still plausible and executable. At the first sign of doubt, they'd search for specific measures that would get the division on track to achieving the targets.

Cash flow and margins began improving within a year. By early 2004, KLM Cargo was a leading player in the worldwide industry and gaining market share. Its margins were acceptable, as were cash generation and return on capital—even in an economic downturn. The improved financial performance allowed it to acquire new and more efficient freighters to further increase market share and improve margins, asset utilization, and cash flow. And because the management team practices the business model drill regularly, all of its members are not merely masters of their functional silos but are well versed in the totality of the business.

MODELING THE SOLUTION FOR KLM

External Realities: The marketplace was not ready for the logistic services the strategic planners hoped to offer. But there was opportunity in the core air cargo business, where some of KLM's competitors managed to make money.

Financial Targets: Cash flow was negative and return on capital close to zero, revenues were flat, and the division was barely breaking even on margins.

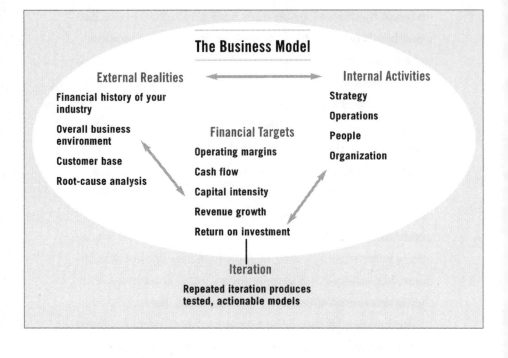

The Business Model

External Realities ←——————→ Internal Activities

Financial history of your industry

Overall business environment

Customer base

Root-cause analysis

Financial Targets

Operating margins

Cash flow

Capital intensity

Revenue growth

Return on investment

Strategy

Operations

People

Organization

Iteration

Repeated iteration produces tested, actionable models

Internal Activities: The idea people who were advancing the strategy lacked operating skills and didn't pay enough attention to the financial targets. Their huge, long-term logistics project was consuming resources without generating growth.

Iteration: Searching for the right mix of elements in the three components, Wisbrun pinpointed the flaws in the existing strategy: it was out of step with current market realities and imposing a prolonged drain on financial resources. In his first iteration he assessed the prospects for a new strategy—return to the core business—and focused on people, creating a new management team to help him determine the requisite changes in people and operations. He and his team then established realistic financial targets, and revisited the model every six weeks to ensure that they were building harmony among the components and on track to meeting the targets.

VANISHING ADVANTAGE

The necessity of a robust and up-to-date business model is heightened in times of structural change like the present. In industries ranging from automobiles and airlines to telecommunications and pharmaceuticals, leaders are asking the same old questions: How should we change our strategies? What's the next wave? Should we be a consolidator or consolidatee? Some, like autos and airlines, have been at it for decades. Yet they keep on coming up short: all their efforts are futile.

The business model helps you understand whether your business's ups and downs are the result of cyclical change, such as demand imbalances resulting from strengthening or weakening of the economy, or structural changes that can have a permanent impact on the profitability of any business.

The evolution of the personal computer industry offers a lesson in the market dynamics that force changes in business models. To date, three distinctly different business models have dominated the industry—possibly a record for one business sector over the course of two decades.

During the 1980s it became apparent that falling technology costs could lead to a large market for personal computers, assuming the computers could be operated by nonexperts. Steve Jobs was the first to aim at this market with desktop machines that any layman could use. Apple Computer, under Jobs's leadership, essentially created the

PC industry with a business model that was initially quite sound. The model was to sell highly advanced, easy-to-use computers to individuals and institutions, especially in education. High margins and healthy asset turnover would generate the cash to fund the R&D that underwrote its strategy: capturing the imagination and building the brand with exciting new products. To protect its position, Apple kept its software and hardware proprietary.

Apple's key operating activities were centered in R&D and product development. Its people were highly creative, technologically advanced product designers, ardent disciples of the charismatic and innovative Steve Jobs. Its somewhat haphazard organizational processes were fairly typical of an early-stage entrepreneurial company. The financial targets, strategy, and operations all worked together as a business model because the company was the only game in town if you were looking for exciting, user-friendly computing. Apple grew rapidly with a great brand and a great return to shareholders.

Then the game changed dramatically and abruptly. IBM entered the marketplace with a different business model: it outsourced production of components for its new PCs, and equipped them with Microsoft's Windows operating system. Bill Gates had designed Windows so that other software makers could create programs for it. Neither Microsoft nor Intel, which supplied the chips, had signed exclusive sales contracts with IBM.

So now anybody who wanted to build computers–even an individual in a garage or college dorm room–could assemble off-the-shelf parts and sell his machines at significantly lower costs than Apple or even IBM. And anybody with an idea for a useful software application could join the party. The PC market exploded: offerings multiplied, and costs dropped to a degree never before seen in a consumer product. Apple's business model was demoted from that of the industry leader to one for a niche player.

The third seismic shift began without fanfare in 1984 when a college student was testing a new business model for PCs from his—yes—dorm room. Michael Dell figured that he could make money building and selling computers at lower cost than the established players by buying off-the-shelf components and taking orders directly from business customers, inviting them to specify the performance and features they wanted. As he prospered, he developed his idea into a unique business model based on high velocity and low margins. Building to order swiftly, he could operate on razor-thin inventory levels. He further ensured high asset efficiency by getting payment before shipping. By the mid-nineties, he was deeply undercutting all of the other major PC makers, and grabbing market share relentlessly.

Dell's business model made all others in the industry obsolete. Today Dell's gross margin and velocity, or revenues per dollar of capital investment, are the highest of any PC maker. Its inventory velocity, or revenues per dollar of inventories, is an astounding 100—nobody else is even close. Result: Dell has cash coming in faster than any of its rivals. At the beginning of 2004, it was generating more than a billion dollars a quarter of cash flow. And it continues to widen the distance between it and other players through constant refinement of its operating activities, people, and organizational processes.

Everything Dell does is driven by the basic business model; nothing has deviated from it. The major operating activity is the supply chain. Nobody matches the speed and efficiency of Dell's sophisticated extended-enterprise manufacturing system; and its extensive customer databases help it market very cost-effectively. Strategically, Dell has expanded the reach of its business model to include servers, storage systems, printers, and consumer electronics items such as TV monitors and digital cameras. The company's organizational processes are heavily based on metrics. They are totally online and transparent, so people in the organization know where they are at any given time and can execute aggressively day by day.

Dell's people are top-notch. Kevin Rollins, Michael Dell's successor, is well matched to the job, and the company is continuously recruiting people with the requisite skills to carry out the strategies and operating activities that support the business model. Competitors have a hard time recruiting people from Dell and none as yet has been willing or able to adopt its model.

A sound business model that links the external environment with right strategy, operating activities, people selection and deployment, and organizational processes is hard to beat. The total package can drive changes in an entire industry and cause others' business models to become obsolete—when, for instance, margins are permanently reduced because of an innovation in the supply chain or in selling. Others may have to incur losses to stay in the game, or will have to get out of the game completely.

BUSINESS SAVVY: PUTTING THE BUSINESS MODEL TOGETHER

As we noted earlier in this chapter, astute leaders of businesses, from the simplest and most primitive to the biggest and most complex, have always had business models in their minds. Until recently they didn't label them as such—the label didn't exist. (Michael Dell once told us, "When I realized that I was suddenly competing in the big leagues, I got scared to death that I wouldn't be able to do it. I didn't recognize my model—I was driven to it!") But they had the focus on the fundamental hows of making money that a business model specifies.

We'd argue that this is the bedrock of the shrewd instinctual feel for how to make money that people call business savvy. It's the ability to make trade-offs among the three components of the business model and match them instinctively and iteratively with the specific actions that create value for customers, owners, and employees.

It's no fluke that business-savvy leaders such as Warren Buffet tend to do these things using the plain language of the shopkeeper: these leaders are in touch with the most fundamental of business fundamentals. A shopkeeper has to navigate his business model and make trade-offs every day. If particular merchandise is not selling, he has to decide whether to cut the price and take the losses in order to generate the cash he needs to pay the lender and buy merchandise to sell the next day. His decisions are no different from those of the automotive executive who has to consider offering incentives on a slow-selling model in order to generate cash.

It takes intense mental activity to reduce corporate-level complexity to the language of a shopkeeper. But now that the business model has a name and a well-developed methodology, there are no more excuses. Business savvy is available to anyone with the mental capacity to anchor his or her thinking in the business model, and to continually gauge the model's health in the context of new realities. You can develop your business savvy through consistent, tenacious practice.

If your business model is faulty, you must think about how you will design a new one. Or if the business model is good and robust but is not delivering the expected results, then you must ask the important question, What is at fault? Is it the strategy, is it the mix of financial targets, or is it an operating activity or a combination of some of them? You must search creatively and aggressively. If the strategy and the operating activities are sound, maybe there's a mismatch in the leadership genes—the wrong people are in charge. Maybe they no longer fit the new reality. Or maybe the organizational processes have become obsolete. If they have not been renewed, one or more may be falling short. Is one of the organizational processes causing good leaders to be consumed in the company's power politics?

The business model is your connection with reality. When you've done your iterations, linking your assessments of the external environment and your internal activities to your hoped-for financial targets, you may or may not like the results you end up with. But you'll be operating in reality rather than in the land of wishful thinking, and you'll be in a far better position to deal with the future before it overtakes you.

part III

What to Change and What Not to Change

Businesses will increasingly find themselves dealing with external forces they didn't foresee. To seize opportunities or defend themselves, they'll have to change faster and more often. But *what* should a business change? How much should it change, how soon and how fast?

There is no one-size-fits-all plan of action. What's right depends on the particulars of your business environment, financial targets, and internal activities—in short, a thorough assessment through the lens of the business model. Not every business model needs an overhaul. Sometimes a company is simply underperforming in a world of opportunity. That's when leaders have to think hard about how performance links with external realities and internal activities, and be judicious in the actions they recommend. The ability to zero in on precisely the parts of the business that need attention and leave the rest alone is just as much a sign of great leadership as is reinventing the business model when radical action is needed.

While some leaders fail to confront reality and avoid change at all cost, others are seduced by it. This is especially the case with the U.S. where culturally, change is as American as apple pie, and laws and customs give companies a flexibility that European competitors can only envy. U.S. companies can acquire or divest businesses with relative ease, restructure, raise productivity by almost any means, reallocate assets, change cultures: in effect, do just about whatever they need to adapt to new circumstances. And most of Asia is closer to the U.S. model than the European one.

Unfortunately, some companies have a tendency to go overboard in exercising this freedom. Too often, decisions about what to change and how much to change are dictated by a leader's personal appetite for it. Magic buzzwords such as *revolution* and *reinvention* fire leaders' imaginations and inspire massive upheavals. Capital markets and the business press act as cheerleaders: big change is good, or at least it's a good story. But change for the sake of change does enormous damage, draining energy and resources from the organization.

Just as often, change is reactive. Especially when they're coming into a new situation, many leaders are anxious to make their mark by making bold, headline-grabbing changes to the financial goals, strategy, organizational structure, and executive team, even when the real problems call for more incremental solutions. Many others stay in their comfort zone by applying what has worked for them in the past, even when those things have nothing to do with the business model at the new company.

The business model brings rationality to the issue of change. It is the guide for when to change and when not to change, what to change and what not to change. If you link your assessment of the external environment to your financial targets and your internal capabilities, you will have a much clearer picture of the magnitude of change required: whether it's a change in strategy, a change in operations and/or people, or a change in the business model itself.

Tools and techniques abound for changing particular components of the business model or the elements within them. Consultants, academics, and experienced practitioners have a tremendous wealth of knowledge on things like strategy, productivity improvement, and customer relations. The harder fix is to the business model itself. Sometimes leaders recognize that they need a new one but can't come up with a business model that hangs together. If every iteration fails, and no other player in the industry has a good one either, it could be that the industry is structurally defective. Frankly, we don't have much advice for companies stuck in a defective industry, especially if their resources have been seriously depleted over time. Your best hope is to see the trouble coming and move out fast.

Use the business model to identify and anticipate external realities and make realistic, positive change. In the following chapters, we look at leaders who have done just that. We begin with three victims of the same calamity, the great tech meltdown. EMC, Cisco, and Sun were all hit hard but differently, and their leaders responded differently. Then we look at 3M, a company that faced no crisis but needed judicious change to improve its performance without damaging its soul. Home Depot, by contrast, had lost its powerful momentum of the nineties, and needed gut-wrenching change. Thomson Corp., our final change story, changed itself most of all—which is really remarkable, since it was under no immediate pressure to do so. But its CEO, looking around the corner, saw better opportunities and went after them.

CHAPTER 6

Facing Crisis: What EMC and Cisco Did That Sun Didn't

The tech boom's collapse created monumental problems for the legions of companies whose business models were predicated on high growth. Many, of course, were doomed even before the meltdown because they were built on insubstantial foundations. But for those that had flourished because their products met real needs, the future depended on how skillfully their leaders adapted to the shock.

We focus on three of the latter, all outstandingly successful during the boom. EMC and Sun found themselves facing structural change in their external environment. While EMC chief Joseph Tucci quickly faced the facts and reinvented his business model, Sun's Scott McNealy struggled to keep on his old course. Cisco's John Chambers realized that his problem was not structural but cyclical and operational. He had to put his company through profound change, but his business model remained intact.

EMC

When Joe Tucci arrived in 2000 as chief operating officer, EMC was riding a rocket. Revenues had risen from $190 million in 1990 to $6.7 billion, and would rise another $2.1 billion in 2000. Its stock price had the highest single-decade percentage increase of any listed stock in the New York Stock Exchange's history.

Anybody who wanted virtually failure-proof storage for vast amounts of data during the late 1990s went to EMC—nobody else could match its technology. It had an estimated 75 percent of the high-end storage market with its Symmetrix, priced from $3 million upwards. EMC had high fixed costs but no competition to speak of; it generated a lot of cash, managing better than 60 percent gross margins and 25 percent operating profits. The three components of the business model were in perfect harmony, with operating activities, selection of people, and organizational processes that reinforced the company's edge in the market. The company earned its margins by spending heavily both on developing cutting-edge technology faster and better than its rivals, and on a top-notch direct-sales force that drove relentlessly to gain and keep market share. A quarterly discipline governed the company's operations and sales: goals, rewards, and even bonuses were based on quarterly financial targets.

As 2001 began, EMC was supremely confident about the future. Though competitors such as IBM and Hitachi were moving upward from their low end of the market, EMC was convinced it was a year ahead of them. Then came the collapse. During the first quarter, sales fell off a cliff, taking profits and margins with them. When the quarterly review came around and Tucci met with his top managers and engineers, almost all of whom had grown up in EMC, they were shell-shocked. Still, they were certain they faced nothing more than a V-shaped blip in the growth curve. Orders were simply being delayed, they figured, because customers had temporarily curbed spending.

EMC's aggressive sales force talked regularly with information technology people at the customers' organizations, but they weren't in the best position to get to the reality of the situation. For one thing, the people they dealt with were fairly low in their organizations and didn't immediately know what their top executives were thinking. For another, EMC's superior technology and past success had persuaded the sales force they were on a team destined to win. Ever optimistic and eager for signals that sales were reaccelerating, they had a bias toward hearing good news. And EMC's quarter-by-quarter focus had them thinking in terms of months rather than looking for structural change in the customer's capital expenditure patterns.

Tucci wasn't so inclined to brush the problem off. He had been through something similar when he was at Wang Laboratories. In the 1980s, Wang stuck with its high-end, high-margin products long after the PC made them hopelessly pricey. After the company went bankrupt, Tucci was named CEO, patched Wang up, and sold it. He wasn't sure whether EMC was in the midst of a cyclical slump or a structural change, but he was determined to find out. "We've got to assume at least a one-year downturn," he told his team. "And in these moments, great companies look in the mirror and become brutally honest. They commit to doing the hard things, as opposed to just trying to cut costs and shuffle their way through the Street's expectations."

The facts he needed to make that judgment lay outside EMC's four walls. While customers were obviously slashing their IT budgets, it wasn't clear at first whether they were simply postponing expenditures. Tucci did not waste time guessing or waiting for sales to pick up again. He went straight to the source, the CEOs and CFOs to whom CIOs at his customers' organizations report and the consultants who advised them, to understand where demand for his products was going. What he heard was eye opening. The collapse of tech spending was real, and there was no reversal in sight. In the face of an economic slowdown, and awash with excess capacity in telecom, customers were making radical changes in how they did business. With pinched margins and dwindling cash, the customers would no longer pay premium prices for top performance. Nor would they stand for proprietary software anymore—they wanted software that could link storage devices from different makers.

Conversations with key decision makers brought to light another external reality Tucci couldn't ignore: IBM and Hitachi were now moving aggressively into EMC's space, selling machines with much or most of the performance of the Symmetrix line but at far lower cost. Customers were flocking to competitors, many with sighs of relief after being beaten up for years by EMC's killer salespeople. Tucci added a few more pieces to the puzzle based on his assessment of technology trends: Hardware costs would continue to drop, as they had in all forms of information technology, and customers would always have a need for service that transcended any single supplier's equipment.

As the final pieces fell into place, Tucci gained confidence in his view of the new external realities. EMC no longer owned its market. The game of high-cost technology, high prices, and high margins was over. The new game wasn't just hardware but also–increasingly–software, service, and solutions. In short, he saw that the existing business model was dead. Each component would have to be reinvented. The challenge was daunting but necessary. "Companies that are afraid to disrupt themselves constantly end up being disrupted," he explained.

As Tucci set out to create a new business model, his business environment continued to deteriorate. Storage industry prices dropped by half during each of the next two years. Things only got worse when Hitachi introduced its improved Lightning storage arrays in 2002, which were faster than anything EMC made. Hitachi added a new distribution channel that accelerated its penetration into EMC's customer base. It sold its products not only directly but also through HP and Sun, at roughly half the price of EMC machines. EMC's share of the high-end market fell from 52 to 41 percent and its gross margins shrank to 32 percent. Revenues fell from the peak of $8.9 billion in 2000 to $5.4 billion in 2002, and profits fell from $1.8 billion to a loss of $119 million.

Focused on where EMC was going and sustained by a soft cushion of cash, Tucci took the business model apart and put it back together. The financial targets clearly had to change. To be competitive, he would have to settle for 30 percent margins, at least initially, and focus on generating cash.

Adjusting to the new realities meant changing all four of the internal activities. Tucci, who was named CEO early in 2001, cut 30 percent of the workforce, removed two levels of management, trimmed spending in hosts of areas, halved capital expenditures, and moved to rationalize production by using more common components. EMC also shed unprofitable non-core business lines and worked the supply chain (the company had previously gotten 60 percent of its components from single sources; today most of its businesses have two or three vendors).

The efforts lowered EMC's annualized cost structure by $1.3 billion, increased cash flow by $600 million—and, importantly, helped preserve hardware margin percentages despite lower prices. One thing Tucci did not do was compromise the future: he held R&D expenditures constant; today they're 15 percent of revenues.

In the old business model, 76 percent of revenues came from hardware, 17 percent from software, and 7 percent from services. The new plan aimed to shrink hardware to 45 percent, with software accounting for 30 percent and services 25 percent. To execute it, EMC needed a different organization structure and processes. Tucci split the company into hardware and software businesses and combined professional services and systems engineering into one group. Doing so shifted the mindset, focus, resource allocation, and priorities toward software and services.

EMC also segmented its potential market into high, middle, and low tiers, and began designing product platforms that could satisfy all three with as much commonality as possible. It added distribution, for example, signing on with Dell to sell its lower-tier Clarion storage systems.

Selling different things meant selling in a different way, and required changes in EMC's people. Running just about the only game in town, the salespeople had pretty much told the customers what they were going to get, and how much they'd pay for it. Not surprisingly, they'd acquired a reputation for being arrogant. That clearly had to change.

The company more than tripled its training budget to create a more customer-centric sales force. The aim was to replace the lone hero salesman culture with one based on teamwork. "Communication is all about synchronization and harmony—understanding the benefits to the customer, and synchronizing processes, vision, mission, and culture," says Tucci. EMC created cross-functional "business management teams" for each product group, aligning product, sales, and marketing people from the outset of the design process. New quarterly business reviews brought all the players together to discuss such matters as pricing, customer value, and how to optimize marketing dollars, and probe for things the company wasn't doing that it should be doing.

One of the toughest issues Tucci faced was the reality that some people who had been key to EMC's past success were not cut out for the demands of the new business model. Among those who couldn't make the shift quickly enough were two trusted members of the senior management team; Tucci had to ask them to leave. Others openly challenged his view of the business environment and refused to buy in to the new model. But Tucci—who didn't lack emotional strength—confronted the painful people issues head-on. He recognized that the various components of the business model had to be consistent with each other: the people had to be suited to the new strategy, organizational structures and processes, and financial goals.

By the beginning of 2004, EMC was growing at twice the rate of its market. Its $1.3 billion acquisition of Legato Systems greatly strengthened its software capabilities, and a partnership with Houston's BMC Software gave it new strength in systems management. The company's aim now, says Tucci, is to "enlarge the pie and get a bigger slice of the larger pie." EMC's competitors, of course, have exactly the same goal. But on the evidence to date, EMC is well into a transformation that will make it a tough foe to conquer. By recognizing the need for a completely new business model and understanding how to link the various components of the new one, Tucci has saved his company from obsolescence and given it a second chance.

MODELING THE SOLUTION FOR EMC

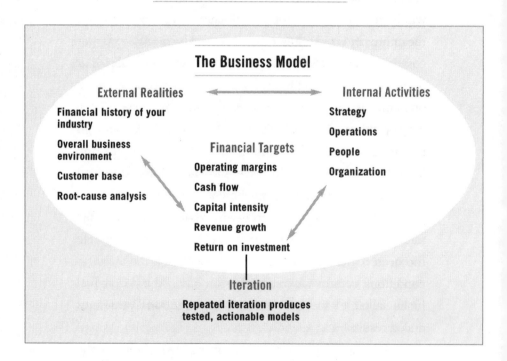

External Realities: After the tech crash, purchasers of storage systems cut back on expenditures and switched from EMC's high-cost products to cheaper ones. Competitors were also developing machines for the high end, at lower cost.

Financial Targets: Revenues, margins, profits, cash flow, and return on investment were all falling precipitously.

Internal Activities: EMC was geared toward producing premium-priced products with proprietary software and high margins. Its technologists strove to design and build highly sophisticated machines; salespeople, operating as loners, were aggressive because they had the most desirable products on the market.

Iteration: Tucci's external analysis showed that the old strategy was obsolete because the market changes were structural. The financial targets could not recover without a whole new business model. He started with a new strategy: recapture and expand the customer base by selling lower cost hardware, software–open, not proprietary–and solutions. The strategy, in return, required major changes in operating tactics, people, and organization processes to develop products at lower cost and more quickly. He and his management team met frequently to iterate in their search for solutions. The first iteration, for example, still left too much high end product to meet the targets for costs, margins, and profits, and led to further work to produce for the middle and lower markets. Subsequent iterations revealed the need to replace people who couldn't adapt to the new conditions, retrain others, and restructure the organization. Financial targets were revised upward as the action plan produced results.

CISCO SYSTEMS

Among the many players humbled in the stock market by the tech meltdown, Cisco stood out for the magnitude of its fall from grace. At its zenith in 2000, the maker of routers and switchgear briefly had the largest market capitalization in the world: at more than $531 billion, it was greater than that of GE, which had six times Cisco's revenues.[1] By mid 2001 Cisco's stock had fallen from its peak of $82 to around $20, eventually bottoming out at around $8 in October 2002.

Cisco's revenues actually increased between 2000 and 2001, from about $18.9 billion to $22.3 billion, before dropping back to roughly $19 billion in the next two years. But the financial markets were expecting continued blazing growth, and when CEO John Chambers appeared to be brushing off his problems they weren't quick to forget their dashed hopes and there was no question that Chambers had a problem on his hands. The evidence was clearest in the first component of the business model. The telecom industry, which accounted for much of his sales, was crippled by overcapacity. Demand was evaporating as the telecoms underwent structural change, and Cisco's profits were evaporating with it.

The bleak prospects might have been enough to panic some leaders into trying to reinvent their business models. Indeed, that's what investors and the business press seemed to be expecting; they all but booed him when he argued that Cisco would weather what he called "a hundred-year storm." But Chambers had looked carefully at his model. Though he recognized that Cisco was hurt, he had reason to maintain his famous optimism.

The model had long been admirable. The linkages between the external environment, the internal activities—particularly its strategy—and the financial targets had made the company a standout. Its highly desirable products were aimed at market segments that were exploding with growth, and while they were competitively priced, they earned attractive margins. Cisco kept up with demand through a strategy that relied heavily on subcontracting, and the low capital intensity in combination with reasonably good margins translated into lofty returns and huge cash generation. The torrid revenue growth earned Cisco a triple-digit price earnings ratio (a company's stock price divided by its earnings price share), and Cisco used its market value as currency to acquire companies for their new technologies, all the while hoarding the huge amounts of cash that flooded in.

What exactly had changed since then? In his root-cause analysis, Chambers reasoned that the telecom business wouldn't disappear forever; it was just getting smaller. There was nothing ominous on the regulatory or competitive fronts, and Cisco's technology was still cutting edge. So for Cisco, this was a nasty cyclical downturn, nothing more.

The financial targets were obviously in trouble at the moment: profits were plunging, and in 2001 the company lost more than $1 billion. But Cisco's cash hoard allowed Chambers to take a bold and savvy $2.5 billion inventory writedown without serious damage. As he continued to revisit the targets, he saw ways to improve margins at lower revenue levels, and to get ready for higher targets when the economy came back. The answer lay in improving cost performance and productivity.

Turning to the internal activities component, Chambers cut nearly 20,000 employees, and slashed the numbers of suppliers and resellers. He rationalized his huge proliferation of products, reducing the lines from 50 to 40 and axing hundreds of models within them. Switches and routers were redesigned for lower cost, using fewer parts, including many that were common among different lines and models. Cisco had acquired hundreds of companies during the boom; Chambers reorganized to integrate the many that were still only half-digested. Finally, he consolidated R&D, which had mainly been conducted at individual product lines, and refocused it to develop more new products internally rather than relying on acquisitions.

Meantime Chambers was looking at the strategy element. He believed he could leverage Cisco's business model in new market segments, especially those where other well-established competitors had come close to bankruptcy. Identifying several markets and segments with high potential, he not only attacked markets for routers and switches, such as the cable industry, but also began increasing Cisco's offerings to include consumer products.

Unlike Joe Tucci at EMC, Chambers did not have to reorganize his company, change his basic product mix, and redesign his entire approach to the marketplace. By 2003, still using its original business model, the company was making headway in six new product areas it calls Advanced Technology markets: optical, network security, IP telephony, wireless LAN, storage networking, and home networking. Each of these, Chambers has said, has "the potential to eventually create a $1 billion revenue opportunity for Cisco." Regardless of how well or poorly Cisco capitalizes on them, they're opportunities that exist only because Chambers made the right decisions when calamity struck. It's hard to know where the company would have been if he had misdiagnosed the change as structural and turned the whole business model upside down instead of focusing incisively on the key elements of the three components.

MODELING THE SOLUTION FOR CISCO

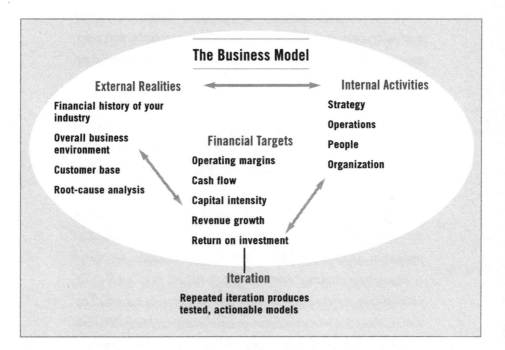

The Business Model

External Realities ⟷ **Internal Activities**

External Realities

Financial history of your industry

Overall business environment

Customer base

Root-cause analysis

Financial Targets

Operating margins

Cash flow

Capital intensity

Revenue growth

Return on investment

Internal Activities

Strategy

Operations

People

Organization

Iteration

Repeated iteration produces tested, actionable models

External Realities: Demand plunged as customers cut back their purchases and confronted the mounting overcapacity in their industry. But Cisco's cutting-edge products were still desirable.

Financial Targets: Revenue growth stalled, margins shrank, and cash generation slowed.

Internal Activities: Cisco's operations and organizational processes were designed for high growth. Product proliferated, and controlling costs was not a high priority.

Iteration: When he read the market downturn, Chambers correctly analyzed it for Cisco, it was cyclical, not structural. He kept his financial targets and strategy intact, and modeled ways to align them with the new and future marketplace realities. After establishing the likely volume of sales, he searched continually and repeatedly for ways to lower costs and get his desired margins. In subsequent iterations, Chambers saw opportunities to get into new markets and segments vacated by fallen competitors; with plenty of cash, he moved to exploit these opportunities.

SUN MICROSYSTEMS

Sun Microsystems is the most puzzling of our calamity trio. By all accounts and evidence, Sun emerged from the tech meltdown sorely in need of a new business model. CEO Scott McNealy stuck with the old one. Bad judgment? Perhaps, but given his history of bucking the odds, we can't write off his chances of recovering.

McNealy, who founded the company at the age of 27 in 1982, created a marvel of innovation, often defying conventional wisdom and succeeding. After a decade of building engineering workstations, he went head-to-head in the server market against IBM, Hewlett-Packard, and Digital Equipment in what was seen as a foolhardy move. But his proprietary chips and architecture delivered unmatched performance, and Sun became the leader in selling powerful, highly secure computers to Internet, telecom, and financial companies. In the mid-nineties he embraced the Java programming language, again successfully bucking the conventional wisdom; Sun made Java an Internet standard.

Sun's business model, like EMC's, was built around producing highly differentiated products and selling them at a premium price that generated fat profit margins. The model supported the company's intensive innovation, and re-warded shareholders handsomely. At the end of 2000, Sun had revenues of more than $18 billion and net income of $1.85 billion; its stock had soared more than sixtyfold in five years, to about $63. Then the collapse put the old model under heavy assault. Customers became much more cost-conscious. They shifted their spending to competitors who sold very good performance at much lower prices, using cheaper chips from Intel and software from Microsoft that delivered performance comparable to that of Sun's costly machines.

Though his sales were plunging, it took McNealy a long time to react. In May, 2002 he finally acknowledged that Sun needed to change. By that time, revenues had fallen to under $3 billion and the company was losing money heavily. Over the next sixteen months, Sun cut costs, introduced lower-priced models, simplified product offerings and pricing, and developed new marketing and sales strategies. For example, though he'd often scorned rivals such as Dell for not inno-vating and instead using other companies' technologies, he began to market low-end servers using Intel chips and the ever-more-popular low-cost Linux software. Indeed, Mc-Nealy has now become a crusader for lower software prices, offering increasing numbers of Linux-based products and even steeply discounting Sun's own Solaris.

Yet at the same time he has stuck resolutely with his vision of continuing to innovate, with an R&D budget of nearly 16 percent of revenues–by far the highest among major com-puter makers.[2] He struck an alliance with AMD to produce high-performance servers with advanced 64-bit technology, something Intel doesn't have, priced aggressively. With a huge installed Java base in cellphones, he laid plans to develop Java-based systems for delivering music, video, and other digital content securely to PCs. Niagara, a chip Sun plans to release in the next two years, is a complete rethinking of how processors work, and the buzz in Silicon Valley is that it could prove to be at least fifteen times more powerful than the most powerful current chips.[3]

How well do these changes confront the realities of Sun's situation? A decade earlier, McNealy dealt with the challenge from servers by moving swiftly to abandon workstations before his market share eroded. This time he reacted late, on the defensive, and without the commanding technological edge he had in the past.

Sun in early 2004 was showing revenue gains, shrinking its net loss, and had some $5 billion in cash. Analysts who the year before had all but given up on the company were backpedaling—just a bit. Sun's stock price was still dawdling in the low single digits, and the consensus was that 2004 would be the make or break year for the company's slightly revamped business model. But not many leaders would choose to take the kind of gambles Scott McNealy relishes. By failing to narrow his choices earlier, he put his company at risk of having few or no attractive options if his luck doesn't hold.

MODELING THE SOLUTION FOR SUN

External Realities: As with EMC, Sun's customers deserted its high-priced, high-performance products after the tech bubble burst, and looked instead for cheaper alternatives.

Financial Targets: Revenues plunged, and margins collapsed; cash generation slowed drastically.

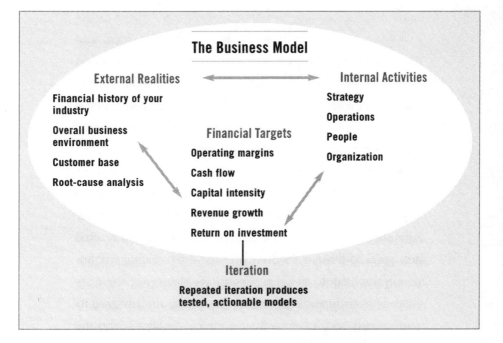

Internal Activities: Sun maintained its technological leadership with intense R&D efforts. Its people and organizational processes were geared to selling unique and demonstrably superior products.

Iteration: Judging the market change as cyclical, McNealy at first stuck to his original strategy and focused on cutting costs with the hope of eventually getting back to his financial targets. As it became apparent that the changes were structural, he went through many iterations to find other ways to meet the target, including broadening his market with lower-priced models, pooling his resources with other technology suppliers, and moving toward open architecture in some product lines. At the same time he has continued on his traditional course, spend heavily on R&D to develop dazzling new technologies over the long haul.

■ ■ ■

WHILE JOE TUCCI, John Chambers, and Scott McNealy responded differently to the industry shakeup they faced, there are common lessons to be learned from their experiences. First, in a time of crisis it's absolutely essential to understand the environment as it has become and is likely to be, rather than what it has been. Second, you need to thoroughly refresh your understanding of your customer base before you decide what actions you're going to take. Third, you must ruthlessly assess your organization: does it have the talent and attitude needed to drive the required changes? If not, what must you do to be sure you have the right people deployed? Fourth, be rigorous in measuring the progress of your turnaround, keeping an eye out for any sign of slippage from the chosen path.

Finally, and above all, approach any crisis without preconceptions: this is the time when relying on the past or on conventional wisdom can lead you rapidly to disaster.

CHAPTER 7

Rebuilding the Foundation
Home Depot

Home Depot roared its way through the nineties on the kind of growth trajectory associated more with a high-tech hotshot than a retailer of lumber and hardware. Arthur Blank and Bernie Marcus, its entrepreneurial founders, were merchandising whizzes with tremendous drive, who created and nurtured an entrepreneurial culture that developed loyal and energetic employees. They seemed to be building the Wal-Mart of home improvement. Home Depot's double-digit revenue growth propelled its stock ever upward; an investment of $100 at the beginning of the decade was worth almost $4,000 at the end.

Then the rocket fizzled out. In 2000, same-store sales declined, the company issued a profit warning, and the stock plunged. Growing competition from Lowe's was taking a toll, but the problems were deeper. Organizational processes had lagged behind the growth, and cash was dwindling. In December the board of directors brought in Robert Nardelli as CEO to straighten the company out.

The choice stunned a lot of people. Investors were disappointed because Nardelli was not a retailer but an industrial guy—he'd previously run GE's Power Systems business. Employees were dismayed because in their eyes, nobody could take the place of the revered Arthur and Bernie. For the next three years, Nardelli would face skepticism and outright hostility from both camps. But what the critics couldn't see at the time was that he had business savvy—and it made all the difference between failure and success.

Nardelli used the business model as his mental framework, scrutinizing each of the three components. The external environment didn't seem problematic. Data on new family formation, housing turnover, and the like persuaded him that while a temporary economic slowdown might dampen sales somewhat, low interest rates and continued strength in the housing market made Home Depot's estimated $900 billion market space an attractive place to be. Lowe's was clearly a threat to be taken seriously; though still half the size of Home Depot, it was gaining market share with bigger stores designed to attract women shoppers, a segment Home Depot hadn't courted much. But it wasn't about to make Home Depot's business model obsolete.

The financial component, however, was badly out of balance. Home Depot had relentlessly been pursuing top-line growth to make its earnings-per-share targets. It was adding some 200 stores a year, handing them over to managers who ran them with almost total freedom. But cash was getting soaked up by inventories and capital expenditures, and sales at stores open more than a year had begun to decline. The cash coffers had to be filled. Expanding beyond 200 new store openings a year, Nardelli concluded, was not realistic unless cash and recruiting of qualified store managers could keep pace.

The connections between the financial targets and the third component of the business model, internal activities gave Nardelli lots to ponder. Compared with GE, the quintessential disciplined company Nardelli was recruited from, Home Depot was an operational free-for-all. The "cowboy culture" that had Home Depot riding high for decades now was running the company ragged. Operations—activities like purchasing, supply chain management, information technology, and logistics, which translate strategy into results—had not become systematized as the company grew from a handful of stores to more than a thousand. (Purchasing, in fact, was called "buying" because Arthur and Bernie thought purchasing sounded bureaucratic.) In Nardelli's words, the twenty-five-year-old company was in start-up mode.

Except for the signature orange aprons that associates on the floor wore, the stores were almost completely uncoordinated. Suppliers were selling the same merchandise to nine different divisions at different prices, and top merchandising managers operated in a hands-off fashion. The company wasn't using the leverage of its considerable purchasing power to negotiate the best possible deals.

Along with new stores, inventory—too much and the wrong kind—was a drain on cash. Store managers tried to keep the shelves filled but had little information to tell them what was selling and what was collecting dust. Information systems were inefficient and out of step with the business needs. When he first arrived in December 2000, Nardelli couldn't even send an e-mail to all store managers, let alone get aggregate point-of-sale information on a timely basis. In effect, says one director, "we ordered $40 billion worth of merchandise with a system consisting of paper and pencil."

Nardelli found that Home Depot sorely needed leadership development. Its people had an admirable can-do spirit, but the cowboy culture made it hard, for instance, to rein in the mavericks for companywide product promotions or top-down initiatives. Many store managers were inexperienced or just incapable of running stores as they got bigger. Associates were sometimes stacking shelves during store hours instead of helping customers. The company did not have a chief marketing officer or chief human resources officer, and because there were no companywide HR processes, it had no consistency in pay or hiring criteria, and no formalized screening or review processes. Occasionally a manager who did poorly at one store would pop up later running another one.

Nardelli was determined to continue expanding the business, and he saw plenty of opportunities to do so with new segments, formats, and geographies, but he had to make the existing stores more professionally run, more appealing to customers, and more profitable. He was eager to centralize some activities, like buying and marketing, and he wanted to install information systems to make the then $45 billion company more efficient. An automated inventory replenishment system would improve inventory turnover, customer satisfaction, and cash generation. Then came the question, What to do first, second, and third?

As Nardelli iterated the business model, the connections between the various internal activities and financial targets became clearer, and the proper sequencing took shape. Improving cash flow and margins required major changes to the internal activities. Adjustments in strategy could deliver profitable growth, but only if the other internal activities were fixed first. Revisiting the people part of the business model brought another reality to light: the top team lacked some of the expertise to make the necessary changes.

Strengthening senior leadership became a priority and a prerequisite for more centralization of some internal activities.

Nardelli rapidly and massively accelerated investment in information technology for self-checkout stations, along with SAP in finance and PeopleSoft in human resources. But some things had to wait. As anxious as he was to install an automated inventory replenishment system, Nardelli postponed it because he recognized that the organization wasn't ready for it. The company was not accustomed to formal training programs of any kind, let alone training on information technology. Trying to adopt a whole new approach to managing without a critical mass of store managers who could readily understand and accept the changes would almost certainly create chaos. Instead of automating inventory management, he reduced inventories using manual systems while addressing the more fundamental need for organization processes, education, discipline, and accountability.

Within two years Nardelli had a new CFO, new executive vice presidents of merchandising, marketing, and information technology, and a new executive vice president of business development and corporate operations, a position he created—all filled by outsiders. He raised the education standards for store managers, encouraged the recruitment of midlevel military veterans who had received leadership training during their tours of duty, and launched training programs.

With the right kind of people in place, Nardelli was ready to make bold moves in the operations area. He focused on productivity, inventory reduction, and efficiency.

In a 180-degree turn from past practice, he centralized buying (and gave it the more corporate sounding name of "purchasing"). As the improvements translated into cash flow and earnings, Nardelli was able to increase information technology expenditures almost twelvefold.

The changes were anything but smooth. The management turnover at the top created turmoil, and the new disciplined approaches to running the business alienated many longtime employees. Critics complained that he was driving away talented people and ruining the company's vibrant culture. Initiatives went awry because they weren't fully understood. For example Nardelli wanted to generate cash by improving inventory velocity. Some store managers responded by cutting back on their inventories without benefit of detailed sales information; shortages developed and sales suffered.

Concern about a slowdown in new stores challenged the very premise of Home Depot's stock market valuation. Even though earnings were growing and Home Depot was generating more and more cash, investors were hooked on revenue growth, and regarded new store openings as the company's most important performance metric. Between May 2001 and early 2003, Home Depot's stock dropped again, from $52 to $22. Other external constituencies were restless, too. Suppliers, unhappy about the centralization of purchasing, spread negative comments through store managers and the buying organization. The media repeatedly raised questions about whether Nardelli was the right man for the job.

Acknowledging that he'd made some mistakes, Nardelli nevertheless stuck to his business model targets. He tried to get investors to focus on cash and earnings instead of revenue growth alone. And the board continued to back him, because they knew what the company needed and where Nardelli planned to take it. One influential board member, Ken Langone, said publicly that if anything, the company wasn't changing fast enough.

By spring 2004, people were finally noticing Nardelli's accomplishments. In three years, annual sales had grown 42 percent, net earnings had grown 65 percent, and cash had ballooned from $200 million to $2.9 billion despite increased dividends and significant stock repurchases. The stock price had climbed back to the mid thirties and the culture everyone was so afraid of destroying had been synchronized with the rest of the business model. Listing Home Depot as number 22 in the "Business Week 50" in March 2004, the magazine said of the company: "Extensive renovations and repairs are starting to pay off."

MODELING THE SOLUTION FOR HOME DEPOT

External Realities: The company's markets had strong growth potential, but Lowe's was gaining ground.

Financial Targets: Revenues were growing, but cash was low and dwindling.

Internal Activities: Organizational processes and people skills lagged behind growth. Decentralized purchasing added to costs, and information systems were primitive.

Iteration: Looking at the financials, Nardelli could discern the negative consequences of Home Depot's fixation on growth. Cash became his critical priority; he slowed the expansion even though it alienated investors, and focused on

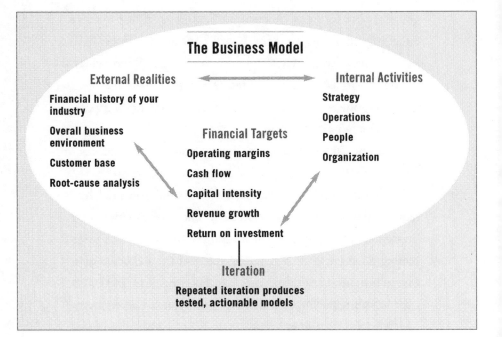

increasing margins by cutting costs and centralizing purchasing. His next steps were to improve management quality and install the information systems needed to manage inventory more efficiently. As these steps generated more cash, he turned to refurbishing the stores and resuming expansion. Periodically, as he gained confidence that his measures were producing results, he was able to raise the long-term financial targets.

CHAPTER 8

Innovating for Growth
The Story of the New 3M

When Jim McNerney was brought in as 3M's new CEO in December 2000, the company had been ambling along with unremarkable earnings, little growth in revenues, and a lethargic stock price. Like many CEO transplants, he could have brought a prepackaged solution with him, raising the bar for financial targets and driving people to meet them. But McNerney was a man with business savvy honed in a wide variety of roles and industries over a quarter of a century, and a master of business model thinking. He took a different course.

3M had a basically sound business model. With a strong culture built on innovation, it did many things extraordinarily well. McNerney recognized that it would be important not to damage that culture. Defining the situation as "a build, rather than a teardown," he concentrated on the third component of the business model to uncover the weaknesses in operations, people, and organization processes that kept the company from realizing its full potential.

He didn't need to spend much time on the first two components of the model. The financial targets would change once 3M started living up to its potential. The business environment was generally attractive, and 3M was well positioned in it, with a mix of businesses and technologies in growth segments such as health care and specialty chemicals used in microprocessors. 3M led in several of its segments, with superb margins, great brands, and proprietary products. Its constant striving for differentiation through technological advances had kept it ahead of the kinds of structural changes that overtook many other companies. In fact, some of its innovations—video tape, masking and cellophane tapes, Thinsulate insulation, surgical drapes—had been game changers, creating whole new industries and spawning whole product families.

To get a handle on the specific things the company had to improve, McNerney spent his first six months in meetings with 3M's senior management—at first the top 20 and later the top 150—a luxury afforded by 3M's good health. As he says, "I had a strong base to build on, and I had a P&L that gave me the time to do it."

He learned the source of 3M's strengths as an innovation machine. Its people, many with long tenure, were talented and hardworking. They placed a high value on independence and the free exchange of ideas, and some longstanding practices reinforced those values. Researchers were allowed to spend 15 percent of their time working on whatever new idea caught their interest, for example, and those at any level were encouraged to call anybody else in the company to further their research interests. And 3M's people were proud; they wanted to win.

The weaknesses also surfaced. The company had no institutional sense of urgency. Projects moved slowly, decisions were made slowly; it took seemingly forever to get a new product to market. For example, the average cycle time for new-product introductions was over four years. Not only had the laissez-faire new product development process lost its discipline and intensity, it was often completely disconnected from marketing. "We discovered we often had inadequate early customer input," says McNerney. "Our default mode was technology all the way up until you built a plant—then you discovered customers didn't want it."

3M was highly decentralized and proud of it. If you want more innovation, break the business into smaller pieces, the thinking went. But one result was a badly fragmented organization: a $16 billion company with forty-five autonomous businesses. Too many units were too small to get any benefit of size and scale, and there was no coordination to leverage their buying power.

The company also lacked disciplined performance reviews and accountability. 3M's pay-for-performance incentive system had deteriorated into a form of entitlement. Business units seldom faced consequences for missing their targets. Lack of differentiation between outstanding performance and mediocrity had the high performers frustrated and provided no real incentive to do things differently.

To generate more revenues, the innovation process had to ratchet up to the next level. The company had to come up with more marketable ideas and commercialize them faster. Marketing and technology had to come together much earlier in the innovation cycle to increase the number of successful new products, and R&D dollars had to be funneled toward the more global projects.

Some fixes were fairly straightforward. McNerney toughened up the incentive system, for example, ensuring that it reflected profit as well as growth by tying a large percentage of pay to economic profit and achieving operating targets.

Besides improving accountability, this helped identify people who had high potential. Those people were pulled out of the ranks and channeled into leadership development programs, where they began to set a faster pace for others.

McNerney grouped the forty-five businesses around markets and customers, and coordinated purchasing across the whole company. But he was careful not to centralize too much. He didn't want to stifle innovation or create a drag on high-growth businesses, and he didn't want to drive away great leaders. Moreover, many of 3M's competitors were small and nimble; if the company became too big and bureaucratic, it could lose its competitive edge.

Changes to the innovation process were close to the heart of 3M, and McNerney proceeded with extra care. Many CEOs in McNerney's shoes would have harangued the organization about the need to focus innovation, do it more productively, and speed up the pace. Then they would have followed up with a series of top-down initiatives to chop out costs, goad people into action, and perhaps layer on a new marketing infrastructure. But McNerney recognized that 3M's proud culture, built through years of success, wouldn't respond well to heavy-handed badgering—especially by a CEO transplanted from GE, a background that can bring a lot of baggage with it.

His challenge was to build the organization's confidence by showing people that they could win, yet instill discipline and rigor and demonstrate a positive role for headquarters. His solution was to launch an initiative that would condition people for change.

He had in mind Six Sigma, which had been a powerful tool at GE for getting people to work together and share best practices. But he put the question to 3M's leaders. The company had pursued process improvement programs before, he noted, but each division chose its own so there was no corporate leverage from any of them. "We're going to pick an initiative so we can all learn from each other," he said. "I would prefer Six Sigma because I know what I'm talking about. If we all want something else, let's pick something else. But let's pick it together and all do it together." It didn't take long for the organization to settle on Six Sigma.

To see it established, he says, "I had to push hard for about nine months. I helped teach the first class to the top 100 guys, and participated with the other infrastructures when they started up, and that got the thing going." As the Six Sigma methodology took hold, decision making became more systematic and disciplined and accountability improved.

In 2001, McNerney geared up to introduce something he labeled "3M Acceleration." The goal, he explained to his organization, was to drive the new product development introduction (NPI) process faster than it had ever been driven. "That captured people's imagination," he says, "because it was built around our fundamental strength of innovation."

No one doubted that the process needed help. Studies showed that for every thousand ideas 3M generated, one hundred were actually launched. To double the number of new products that got launched, then, 3M should double the number of ideas, right? That was assuming that the existing processes were running at optimum efficiency. McNerney knew they were not.

In talking with people at 3M and studying the innovation process, McNerney learned that there were seven distinct steps—idea generation, concept development, feasibility analysis, product development, scale up, launch, and post-launch follow-up. But those steps were really part of two core processes, each of which had very different characteristics and requirements. The genetic code of the idea generators, the people who came up with new ideas but stopped short of developing them, was different from that of the commercializers who turned the ideas into viable products. The ideas that got developed were "selected" by virtue of the idea generator's efforts to push it to the next step. To work best, each group had to be selected, motivated, and rewarded differently.

The acceleration initiative aimed to embed four principles in the NPI process: to let the market, not just the technologists, define the opportunities, to ensure candid market assessments, to make approvals and decisions based on data and facts, and to focus on fewer programs that had higher impact. Letting the marketplace "speak" and using facts to inform decisions about what ideas to pursue based on their likely market impact provided the much-needed discipline and linkage. They were instilled by challenging the R&D leadership to raise the bar on innovation, and to reconnect R&D with the businesses and with customers. In other words, the change process was designed, owned, and implemented by the R&D team—not mandated by the CEO.

With a firm grasp of how the organization could power up its innovation engine, McNerney established goals for accelerating new-product introductions: 3M would double the number of new opportunities it identified and triple the number of products that were actually brought to market in one year. Instead of coming up with 1,000 new ideas, of which 100 were commercialized, the company would come up with 2,000 ideas and bring 300 to market.

Built into the 3M Acceleration initiative was a top-down resource allocation framework. R&D resources had been spread fairly equally across the entire company, so hundred-year-old technologies got just as much R&D as a percentage of sales as did the pharmaceutical business. The divisions that weren't doing so well claimed to need the R&D as much as anyone. They were convinced that they were just months away from innovating their way out of the hole. The new approach allocates resources across divisions based on market opportunities. Healthcare, for example, has grown from about 25 percent of revenues and 30 percent of earnings to 30 percent of revenues and 35 percent of earnings, and the opportunities are huge. Money from the more mature parts of the business is now funneled toward the growth areas.

Though McNerney brought dramatic changes to 3M, its people embraced them willingly because he had spent so much time listening to them. He had made an earnest effort to understand the company's internal realities, listening more than talking and staying open to the opinions of those who lived it on a daily basis. He had to withstand criticism for not making bold moves in his first six months on the job, but the time spent to understand the internal realities paid off.

Other changes followed, including an initiative on leadership, along with an unprecedented degree of centralization. But all derived naturally from looking at the business realistically and through the business model. The results have been clear. 3M shortened the new product introduction cycle by a year and a half. Revenues grew by $1.5 billion from 2000 to

2003, and operating margins rose several percentage points during that period, just shy of the goal McNerney had originally set. The stock price has nearly doubled since he took over, and analysts project that it will double again in two years. McNerney is admired both inside and outside the company.

MODELING THE SOLUTION FOR 3M

The Business Model

External Realities ⟷ Internal Activities

External Realities
Financial history of your industry

Overall business environment

Customer base

Root-cause analysis

Financial Targets
Operating margins

Cash flow

Capital intensity

Revenue growth

Return on investment

Internal Activities
Strategy

Operations

People

Organization

Iteration

Repeated iteration produces tested, actionable models

External Realities: Markets in general were growing well, and there were no dramatic threats on the horizon.

Financial Targets: 3M was meeting all of them, but they were modest and well below the company's potential.

Internal Activities: Talented people made the company an innovation machine. But new product development was disconnected from customers, and took too long. Operations lacked discipline.

Iteration: During six months of meetings with senior management, McNerney searched for ways to improve financial results without damaging 3M's culture of innovation. He repeatedly iterated his approach to change until he was satisfied that he had the right mix and sequence of actions. He then set higher financial targets, transparent both inside and outside the company, and began to change organizational processes, combining many businesses and centralizing such things as purchasing. After conditioning his people for change by introducing a Six Sigma initiative, he overhauled the innovation processes to speed them up and connect them more closely with the marketplace.

CHAPTER 9

Seizing Opportunity: How The Thomson Corporation Transformed Itself

The Thomson Corporation didn't look much like a company in need of transformation when Richard Harrington took over as CEO in 1997. The U.S. $8.8 billion-a-year business had a proud history and enjoyed an almost legendary status. Founder Roy Thomson built it from a single newspaper in a northern Ontario mining town during the 1930s into a holding company that owned an empire of more than a hundred newspapers in Canada, the United States, and Britain, as well as an oil business. Thomson was awarded a peerage for his accomplishments. His son Kenneth, who inherited the title as well as the business, added another 180 papers. Thomson also ran a number of professional publications, which ranged from *Jane's Fighting Ships* and obscure industrial publications to textbooks and journals for medical, legal, health-care, and educational professionals. Finally, it owned a travel and resort business in the U.K. that accounted for a third of corporate revenues. Nevertheless, the newspapers—run with a celebrated frugality—were the fastest-growing chain in North America, and the second most profitable after Gannett.

Overall, revenues were growing about 8 percent a year, compounded. Earnings before interest, taxes, depreciation, and amortization (EBITDA, a measure favored in publishing) were growing at an 11 percent rate; operating income, around 11 percent; and return on invested capital was about 10 percent. Free cash flow was $264 million.

But Roy Thomson's entrepreneurial spirit still shaped the Thomson culture. The Thomson family, which owned 73 percent of the stock, and the board of directors were always looking for opportunities. What's more, they had the confidence and willpower to pursue long-term goals. A couple of years before naming Harrington CEO, for example, they'd sold some of the papers to put more emphasis on developing the professional publications and moving to electronic publishing.

Harrington was a good fit. He had run the newspapers for the previous four years, and before that, the professional publications. A careful observer of the business environment, he had begun to form doubts about the long-term prospects for the newspapers. The business was highly cyclical, for one thing, following the economic ups and downs. More important, he'd noticed that new players outside his industry were shrinking his customer base of advertisers.

Category killers such as The Gap and mass retailers were wiping out department stores in the towns and cities served by Thomson papers. And those stores were major sources of advertising revenues. Harrington could see nothing in sight that would replace them in the papers' profit streams; when the newcomers advertised in newspapers, they used circulars, which were far less profitable than traditional ads. Moreover, classified advertising, which accounted for some 30 percent of the top line and more than half of the bottom line, looked threatened by another new player: Harrington suspected that the rise of the Internet would, over time, capture an increasing share of those ads.

Nor was Harrington confident about retaining the loyalty of readers, the other part of his customer base, over the long run. "The third concern was our value proposition," says Harrington. "We'd done a very good job with our readers and advertisers—that's how we got the growth. But could we continue to build the value proposition day in and day out if the financial model changes? If you had core properties like the *New York Times* or the *Wall Street Journal,* you could probably do something. But if you owned mostly regional newspapers, you didn't necessarily have a way to get out of it."

A lot of leaders at this point would head straight to the third component of the business model and immerse themselves in redesigning the strategy: what could Thomson do to attract new advertisers, say, or increase circulation? Should it be a consolidator, continuing to acquire more papers? That would create growth, and possibly some efficiencies of scale.

But Harrington was looking at the reality of the business model as a whole. His central question was whether a model dependent on regional newspapers would run out of gas no matter what new strategy might be conceived and executed. Linking the trends to Thomson's financial targets, he could see no way that the model could continue to create value for shareholders in the future. Though there might be ways to boost top-line growth, an industry with declining profitability could not meet the targets for free cash flow, EBITDA, and return on invested capital.

The analysis exposed a simple but crucial question, one that business leaders all too often don't get to when they're caught up in the details of strategy: If the model is not adequate for the future, what fundamentally needs to change? What arena can we play in where the business model will create long-term value?

The analysis also highlighted a secondary but not unimportant problem. While Thomson's stock had performed reasonably well, management felt it was undervalued because investors couldn't see a clear focus to the business. For this reason, Thomson had been planning to sell the leisure business. Now a concept with a much sharper focus began to emerge. As Harrington and the others in Thomson's leadership team studied their external landscape and business activities, they could see the outline of a whole new business model.

The specialty and professional publications were then a mixed bag of largely print publications, with some electronic add-ons. Many had been acquired during the course of expansion into the United States according to a strategy that Harrington describes as "Let's get into businesses where the customer is ordering a product that's being paid for by someone else." In the education area, for instance, the professor decides what the textbook is, the bookstore provides it, but the student pays for it. The same with legal and the others—the professional is buying the product and using the research, but charging it off to a third party. The idea, explains Harrington, was that these businesses would be less sensitive to cyclical ups and downs of the economy.

But professional publishing was also a growth business. In an increasingly knowledge-work economy, the thirst for information would grow enormously as more and more of it became available electronically. "We felt that longer term this should really be an outstanding marketplace," says Harrington. "We said, 'We're in these businesses; we know these markets to a degree; we know that these markets should continue to grow, because the U.S. had to really develop the knowledge worker economy. And we knew technology was going to change, which would really change the game.' So from that, we said: 'Okay, what markets are the most robust?' And we had pieces of all of them: legal and regulatory, financial service information, scientific research, health care, and learning."

Harrington and his team concluded that Thomson's new business model would be focused on electronic publishing. They would build an integrated information enterprise that could create real value and meet the financial criteria for long-term success. The board and the family agreed that the risks were well worth taking in light of the opportunity to create long-term value, and backed him enthusiastically.

AN OPPORTUNITY TO TRANSFORM AN INDUSTRY

The proposal was not for the faint-hearted. It would take Thomson out of the business it knew best and at a time when it was at the top of its game and thrust it into a new competitive environment, going head to head with companies like Reed Elsevier, McGraw-Hill, and Wolters Kluwer. All had more depth and breadth of experience in professional publishing. It would also hurt financial results in the short run. The newspapers weren't capital intensive, but expansion would be. Thomson would have to spend a lot of money, including the heavy up-front investments necessary to build an electronic publishing business. Return on capital would be depressed for some years to come. The transformation would also be a huge leadership challenge: new talent would have to be developed, new disciplines learned, and disparate cultures merged into a unified organization.

But in one sense the playing field in its formative phase was more level than it looked. Publishers were just starting to go electronic, and if Thomson could get in on the ground floor and build up rapidly, Harrington believed, it could compete with the best in this new peer group. "It actually gave us an opportunity to not only transform our business," he says, "but to become one of the leaders in transforming the whole industry." If Thomson could do that, the investment would pay off handsomely.

Harrington didn't waste any time. The travel and leisure business went on the block in March 1998, and brought about $2.8 billion, enough to get the transformation started. Completing the sale of the newspapers—some had already been shed—was next in line. There was no financial urgency to sell, and in the boom economy of the late nineties they were generating strong profits. But Harrington gauged that they were probably nearing a cyclical peak. In 2000, he decided it was time to make the move.

"We debated the timing with the board," he says. "We said, 'Let's do it right away. We've had a great economic run, but we have no idea how long it's going to continue. If we wait and fall into an economic decline, we'd be owning them for another seven years.' The board enthusiastically agreed." Needless to say—and to Harrington's continuing satisfaction even today—the timing was all but perfect. All told, the papers brought in 3.3 billion. Thomson also sold all of the specialty publications that didn't fit with the new model.

Shareholders often abandon a comfortable boat when management rocks it, but Thomson's leaders had taken care to explain what they had in mind. The outside investors were happy to see a clear focus, and nudged the stock up. But the next step wouldn't be easy. "We were kind of niche players in most of our target markets, and each of the publishing companies was managed as a stand-alone business," says Harrington. "So the next question was how do we build enough size and scale to become a major player in each of those marketplaces? And how do we become an information-services company, as opposed to an information-publishing company?"

The company created a framework of four strategic market groups, each with a core in its existing competencies—mainly supplying newsletters, databases, textbooks, and the like to organizations and professionals. Legal and Regulatory's main customers include specialists in law, tax, accounting, intellectual property, and compliance; Learning serves secondary, college, and graduate schools, along with professional and corporate training organizations; Financial serves customers throughout the financial services industry; and Science and Healthcare is aimed at researchers, librarians, clinicians, and other professionals.

ANCHORED IN THE BUSINESS MODEL

Over the next several years, Thomson spent some $7 billion to acquire more than two hundred businesses. Building the groups was a major assembly job. "We had to take individual product companies, find out what the issues were in the marketplaces where we wanted to compete, and acquire the right individual product companies to give us the capabilities, size, and scale," says Harrington. "Then we had to retrofit them into a whole new business model."

Acquisition is, of course, a key element of many companies' growth strategies. But the ever-present danger is undisciplined acquisition—the businesses that get picked up in a burst of excitement or unwarranted optimism because the opportunity seems such a good fit with somebody's vision of the possible.

Thomson was very clear about the need for good strategic fit, and the business model provided financial discipline. The major acquired businesses had to be leaders in their fields. They had to be able to be leveraged, both strategically and financially. Strategically meant that they would add specific building blocks or expertise that would contribute to organic growth. Financially, the acquisitions had to be able to soon meet or surpass Thomson's financial targets. The entire transformation phase was always anchored in financial targets, the second component of the business model. Harrington had observed companies that got into trouble when acquisition programs overloaded their balance sheets with debt. He knew the transformation would succeed only if cash flow remained generally robust, so that Thomson would not have to take on mountains of debt to reach its goals.

Thus the model drove the acquisition of companies that were among the top in their businesses, with sound finances and management, that would meet Thomson's return on investment target and yield accretive earnings sooner rather than later. They would also need to fit well with the Thomson culture. "We did an awful lot of work before the acquisitions to know exactly what the integration process was going to be, so that we could pull the cost out of the business as quickly as possible," he says.

Despite the Thomson heritage of frugality, bargain hunting wasn't in the model. "You get what you pay for," says Harrington, adding, "I had a competitor who did the opposite, and they're suffering today for it."

THE HOLISTIC ROUTE TO GROWTH

The growth opportunities came in stages. Historically, publishers such as Thomson existed to supply information. In the early days of electronic publishing, they delivered the traditional print product to the desktop via floppy disks. Then came the Internet, and the value added became speed, currency, and interactivity. In the next stage, the industry began supplying tools and applications that let customers not only get the information but also integrate research, news, intelligence, and databases with their own information.

From the outset, Thomson aimed to sell not just content but everything else that was related. It moved rapidly through this progression as it added companies, expanding each new business into a supplier of integrated electronic solutions. For example, Legal and Regulatory was originally an information provider to law firms—large, medium, and small—and a supplier of textbooks to law schools. In due course its leaders discerned a need among their customers for websites and electronic directories. It began offering them, and by 2003 the website and directory business had grown to more than $75 million. More recently, it's added a product called West Knowledge Management that allows users to search a firm's internal database. Says Harrington: "The key is taking a holistic view of what is going to happen in a law firm: what do they need, and where can we play a role in it?"

No challenge was bigger than developing Thomson Financial. It had grown fast; by 1999 it had more than forty businesses producing information, analytical tools, and workflow systems for the financial services industry, with a combined revenue of about $1.5 billion. Almost all were leaders in their markets, some by a wide margin. For example, 98 percent of institutional money managers and almost all the major newspapers were using Thomson First Call, which summarizes equity analysts' quarterly earnings predictions.[1]

But Thomson Financial was far from holistic. The businesses weren't integrated; each had its own products, processes, systems, and sales force. This loose collection wouldn't be enough to meet the Thomson business model criteria going forward.

"We looked at it and said, in effect, we can't get there from here," says Harrington. "If we were to just continue with individual high-priced products, we'd have too many competitors who could come in underneath us and pick us off one at a time. We could no longer be just content providers; we had to build a lot of tools and applications and aggregate our content." The situation became even more urgent with the market downturn that began the following year. As customers retrenched on spending and turned to cost cutting, revenues declined.

Thomson continued to enlarge Financial's size and scale with such acquisitions as Primark, a major provider of financial data, in 2000. But its main thrust was to knit the businesses together. Thomson Financial's management team consolidated them into three strategic customer units, centered respectively on banking and brokerage sell-side businesses, investment management, and corporate financing. It developed a single, open-architecture electronic infrastructure. It simplified its dozens of product offerings, reducing them to seven integrated solutions packages that can be tailored for each of the company's customer segments. And it wedded customer units with a common sales force that gives large customers a single point of contact.

By 2003 Thomson Financial was able to point to a clear competitive differentiation: the ability to offer total workflow solutions combining information, configurable technology, and integrated applications. A milestone marking the success of this effort came when Thomson beat out Bloomberg and Reuters to develop a new wealth management technology platform for Merrill Lynch. The project was the single biggest information solutions deal ever done in the financial services industry, and Merrill Lynch's first IT outsourcing venture. Its total value was about $1 billion; Thomson's share was $300 million over five years, for providing the systems, serving as general manager in coordinating the other vendors, and ongoing management.

The package included workstations for some thirty thousand Merrill Lynch financial advisors. Their Dell desktops provide them with two screens, one with CRM client information and the other with Thomson's financial information and applications. All are linked into Merrill Lynch's back-end systems and databases, and—of course—to the Internet.

Why did Merrill Lynch choose Thomson? According to Byron Vielehr, co-head and chief technology officer of

Merrill's Global Private Client Group, "The most important driver was the comfort level Merrill execs had with Thomson executives, and Merrill's belief that Thomson's senior management team would stay intimately involved in the project." Also of obvious importance were the company's products and services themselves. But one other item suggests that the much (and justly) maligned word *synergy* is not totally without meaning. Early on, Viehler said, it became clear that training would be a critical issue. As a result, Merrill was pleased that Thomson could bring the expertise developed in its learning group to the project.[2]

A FOCUS ON THE CUSTOMER

Thomson's marketplace successes reflect a powerful focus on customer needs. Harrington sought from the beginning to make Thomson customer-centric. With heavy up-front investments that had to be expensed, it was essential to get scale and volume in a hurry, along with enough pricing power to preserve margins. This would require new skills in analyzing specific customer needs, developing highly differentiated products quickly, and pricing them correctly.

"Understanding our customers' business needs fundamentally drives our strategy," Harrington says. "When we started this transformation and looked at the future—the competitive nature of the business and the changes going on in it—one of our conclusions was, 'Boy, if we're not as good in our front-end customer strategy as some of the best consumer product companies, it's going to be really difficult for us to be number one in our markets.' "

Before Thomson business unit managers even start thinking about their strategies, they are expected to thoroughly understand their potential customers and the customers' needs. After all, says Harrington, "There's no sense doing a strategy unless you understand what you're going after." Thomson makes extensive use of a tool called customer mapping, which lays out a comprehensive view of a market and its segments. Using a customer map, leaders can judge the size of a market's segments and subsegments, see how segments compare with and relate to one another, and pinpoint how their units and their major competitors are positioned in each segment.

Thomson started using market mapping in 1999, when it was trying to get the right focus for Thomson Financial, and the process quickly proved its worth. "It gave us a much better idea of what we were going after—the size of the markets and segments, the areas where we were strong and where competitors were strong. And we also used it to target acquisitions.

"The key is that there's no such thing as a perfect strategy or perfect information. All you can do is be directional, and the mapping gives the good-quality information that gets us in the right direction."

THE SECRET OF SUCCESS IN A CHANGING WORLD

Over the course of its transformation period, Thomson grew its total revenues at a compounded annual rate of 7.4 percent, and its organic revenues at about 5 percent. Though the company could not escape the consequences of economic slowdown in the early 2000s, its 2003 revenues stood just $1.2 billion shy of the 1997 level, before the travel business and papers were sold off. Its EBITDA margin rose from 18 percent in 1997 to 27 percent. Thomson was listed on the New York Stock Exchange in 2002, with an initial market capitalization of $19.5 billion; in May of 2004 it stood at $21 billion. Today Thomson serves more than 20 million users in some 130 countries, and is matched in revenues only by Reed Elsevier. And it is widely acknowledged as the industry leader in transforming itself into a provider of value-added electronic solutions.

Analysts at BNP Paribas Equities tell the story succinctly. "In contrast to most of its peers, Thomson Corp. has handled this transition with the preservation of key valuation metrics and cash returns," they observed in October 2003, "On our calculations, pre-tax ROIC has remained broadly constant at around 8 percent since 1998, compared with relative declines at Reed Elsevier and Wolters Kluwer. A well-managed investment phase and further economies of scale should translate into steady cash flow growth and improved cash returns. We forecast an increase in the company's pre-tax ROIC to close to 12 percent by 2005."[3]

Thomson reached this point because its leaders worked their business model assiduously. They understood the external environment and anticipated the changes that would make Thomson's old business model obsolete. They searched their existing business activities to locate the ones that could be developed to sustain a new business model, and developed the strategies that directed their growth. They built with constant attention to the business model's financial targets. And they executed the organizational and people changes necessary to make the whole transformation work.

Taking risks came more naturally to Thomson's leaders with their eyes on the long run, than to most whose businesses are in apparent comfort zones. But they minimized their risks, and maximized their opportunities, with a well thought out business model. That's a lesson with value for the bold and timorous alike.

MODELING THE SOLUTION FOR THOMSON

External Realities: The newspaper and travel businesses were currently profitable, but the future looked less promising. By contrast, Thomson's smaller professional publishing business appeared to have enormous growth potential.

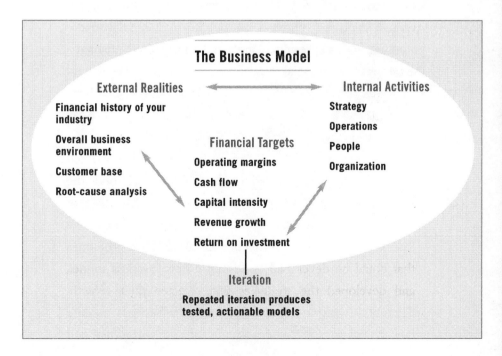

The Business Model

External Realities ⟷ Internal Activities

External Realities:
- Financial history of your industry
- Overall business environment
- Customer base
- Root-cause analysis

Financial Targets:
- Operating margins
- Cash flow
- Capital intensity
- Revenue growth
- Return on investment

Internal Activities:
- Strategy
- Operations
- People
- Organization

Iteration

Repeated iteration produces tested, actionable models

Financial Targets: Thomson was currently meeting its long-run targets. But with the newspaper business, that would not necessarily be the long-term case.

Internal Activities: People, operations, and organizational processes were well harmonized for the existing businesses.

Iteration: Harrington recognized that structural changes would erode the newspapers' profitability, then at their peak. He and his board agreed that Thomson should create an entirely new business model. It would achieve desirable financial targets by publishing (increasingly electronically) information for professionals such as financial services people and lawyers. Harrington first modeled the relationships between different sale prices for the businesses to be sold and the investment required to build professional publishing. Arriving at a balance that would not require heavy borrowing, he proceeded with the plan. As the plan moved forward, it required continual changes in people and organization processes, with the results being weighed constantly against the progress on financial targets.

part IV

How to Prepare for Change

Succeeding in today's business world requires skills and abilities that haven't been given much weight in the past. Acute radar is one of them: you need to "look around corners" and specifically discern the parts of the external environment that will affect the future of your business. Leaders who've learned to look at their businesses from the outside in, including working backwards from the end user of their products and services, have a head start in confronting reality.

No matter how observant their leaders are, though, businesses can't change unless they are conditioned to do so. In our experience, there's no better way for such conditioning than the companywide initiative. These undertakings teach people how to work together in tackling the kinds of challenges that external reality is constantly throwing at you.

Ultimately, the organizations that work most effectively will be those in which leadership demands reality and develops systems of rewards and penalties that put a premium on realism. That premium is more important than ever before, which means that creating a culture of reality moves to one of the top places on any leader's agenda. Realism starts with your own behavior, using the business model as your primary tool for teaching people to confront the realities that affect their area and organizational levels.

CHAPTER 10
Looking Around Corners

The external environment has always thrown challenges at even the best business models, as the stories of companies such as Stanley Works, Kmart, Apple, EMC, Cisco, and Sun illustrate. Conversely, it's always offered opportunities for those able to spot them, like Sam Walton, Bill Gates, Michael Dell, and Thomson's Richard Harrington.

Today the increasing speed and scale of change means that new threats and opportunities arise faster and more often. Shifts in everything from consumer lifestyles to the global financial markets and government regulations can alter not only your own business model but those of whole industries. To take one recent example, in scarcely a year the U.S. low-carbohydrate craze blossomed from a fringe idea into a significant game-changer for food producers and restaurant chains.

How can you anticipate change before it's too late? Is it really possible to know, in Wayne Gretsky's famous phrase, not where the puck is but where it's going to be? The answer is yes, but only if you learn how to look around corners by understanding the realities outside your walls in more breadth and depth than ever before.

Looking around corners is not just the CEO's job, as the story of John P. in Chapter 1 makes clear. In the battle for every point of margin and every cent of cash, the manager of any business unit, product line, or P&L center absolutely must know how to understand the impact of the external environment on her business.

THE AGENTS OF CHANGE

In Chapter 2 we described a business environment of unprecedented change. Maybe you thought it was all a bit "big picture," not something likely to affect you right here and now. So let's first talk about some of the ways it can.

Say you can't get any pricing power today. Is that really because the excess capacity you see is a cyclical issue, or is the business already so overcrowded that nobody can make decent money in the long run? Intel CEO Andy Grove's ability to make that distinction in the 1980s led to one of the most famous business model shifts ever. Memory chips were the foundation of Intel's business, but their prices were dropping precipitously as low-cost competitors in Japan added new capacity. Debates over the cause and response consumed Grove and his management team for months. In the end, they concluded that commoditization was inevitable, and agreed to essentially abandon the business they started with. They redirected their resources into processors, where Intel maintains its differentiation to this day.

As Grove recalled, "I was in my office with Intel's chairman and [then] CEO Gordon Moore, and we were discussing our quandary. Our mood was downbeat. I looked out the window at the Ferris wheel of the Great America amusement park revolving in the distance, then I turned back to Gordon and I asked, 'If we got kicked out and the board brought in a new CEO, what do you think he would do?' Gordon answered without hesitation, 'He would get us out of memories.' I stared at him, numb, then said, 'Why shouldn't you and I walk out the door, come back in, and do it ourselves?'"[1]

With competitive intensity on the rise, more and more products and services are being knocked off or functionally matched, produced somewhere by somebody at lower cost. Sooner or later they're commoditized—and it's usually sooner. Companies everywhere are a lot more nimble than they used to be, thanks both to the power of computing and to successful efforts to streamline management and reduce cycle times. The differentiation vital to wide margins and high profits is harder to achieve, and its lifespan is shorter.

Along with speed comes a higher order of unpredictability. It used to be that you knew your adversaries. Most were competitors not unlike you, in industries not unlike yours, with goals similar to yours. And you had a pretty good idea who you'd be battling in the future—the same crew, maybe some upstarts or foreigners, possibly a disruptive technology. All that has changed dramatically.

Today the next assault on your ability to make money can come from almost anywhere. You have to study your extended industry, which includes all of the players who influence the industry's behaviors and economics. Some are in the industry. Some are elsewhere in your value chain: suppliers, channel partners. Some are in related industries. At any given time some may be adversaries, some may be allies, and some may be neutral. But increasingly—and often when you least expect it—their behaviors can upend your old assumptions.

As we saw in Chapter 2 in the story about Stanley Works, mass channel retailers, among the heaviest players in the new environment, have drastically changed the game for all manufacturers of consumer products. In the good old days, you designed your product, made it, priced it, and sold it to wholesalers or retailers. You had at least some control over what you produced and when, and how much money you made on it. Now retailers like Wal-Mart dictate costs based on those of the lowest-cost producers in the world, and they dictate delivery schedules based on real-time market demands. Often they also dictate design, based on feedback from consumers. And more and more often, they are deciding to deal their traditional suppliers out entirely and develop their own branded goods.

Some of the players you have to worry about aren't in any industry at all—they are governments or players in the capital markets. The agonies of the U.S. telecom industry, depicted also in Chapter 2, come in large measure from two decades of regulatory efforts. Many of these did indeed benefit consumers, as intended. But the damage they caused is exacting a heavy toll of cost and uncertainty among telecom companies. Or consider the aircraft industry, also roiled by government actions. While Boeing's diminished competitive stature owes much to the company's own mismanagement, its troubles began with the decision of European governments to create Airbus Industrie and finance it through years of losses. Look for more such meddling in the years to come: could your industry be next?

Other future concerns could be problems of your own industry's making, the results of past decisions that now come back to haunt you. That's the case with the legacy costs we've mentioned previously–the pension and health benefits promises made in the golden past when unions and management agreed to assume that the future would always be better and richer than the present. It's also the case with investment decisions made during bubbles and booms, where almost everyone becomes persuaded that trees grow to the sky. Apart from saddling companies with debt burdens and collapsed share prices, such overinvestment leaves a hangover of excess capacity that can take a generation or more to wring out.

Nontraditional competitors are perhaps the most numerous of the new players. Companies have, of course, long reached outside their own industries or traditional areas of expertise in searching for new business. Chains like 7-Eleven, for example, saw their competitive environment change for the worse decades ago when gasoline retailers began installing convenience stores on their prime real estate. But today it's routine for players to move into spaces that formerly would have seemed remote: Amazon.com's expansion from an online bookstore to a virtual shopping mall; electronics retailer Best Buy's selling appliances; Dell's growth into the server market, and then into markets for everything from printers to digital cameras (now a challenge to Best Buy); GE's expansion from building aircraft engines into airplane maintenance.

Who, ten years earlier, would have predicted that Wal-Mart in 2003 would be one of America's biggest sellers of groceries, books, and music? Or that Samsung's electronics business, then a producer of low-cost components for the

Japanese, would be a potent brand at the cutting edge of high-style, high-function consumer electronics? Everybody, it seems, wants to go everywhere.

Unexpected competition isn't necessarily the most threatening complication of the new business environment. Some players may not specifically compete with you, but they have the power to change the rules of the game as you've played it previously. Often, their behaviors aren't the ones you take for granted in your own moneymaking scenarios.

TOOLS FOR STAYING AHEAD

How do you know what you need to do before it's too late to do it? In most businesses, people typically look only briefly at what economists call externalities in analyzing their opportunities and risks, and their research consists largely of generic economic and industry growth projections. They put most of their time into studying the strengths and weaknesses of their major rivals. They look for ways to beat the competitors—build new low-cost capacity, develop a new technology, create a new marketing strategy, and so forth. That's what AlliedSignal did, for example, with its automotive unit, as described on pages 73–75. There's no question that competitor analysis is important, but it's only the beginning.

You have to constantly ask the bigger questions: Can you see profitable growth in the industry? What could commoditize it? Can you foresee a technology change (by you or from elsewhere) that might alter the rules of engagement? Who else might become a competitor? What government policies are brewing that could affect you for worse or better? Is the industry structurally defective, or heading that way?

And most important, what do your customers think? We are astonished at how many business leaders fail to understand the wants and needs of the end users who buy their products. These ultimate customers may not see the product differentiation the leaders see. You have to understand how you look through the eyes of the end user.

To know and anticipate these things, you must take information gathering to the next level. You have to use far-ranging inputs to test the validity of the business model and all of the strategies and operational issues that arise from it.

Gathering information from outside is not a onetime or yearly event. It has to be a real-time process: a social mechanism with frequency and consistency. If you do it just during the planning session, that's too late. It has to inform the business model, and all of the daily decisions people make about their direction and processes.

■　■　■

THE ABILITY TO LOOK AROUND corners and anticipate what's coming is part mental and part procedural. The mental part comes from a determination to get to the bottom of things—to ferret out inconsistencies in the linkages of a business model's components, for example. This mindset develops with practice, and people who've developed it pursue problems both consciously and unconsciously until they've found solutions. The procedures consist of a variety of tools for looking from the outside in—but they're only worthwhile if you bring the right mindset for working with them.

If you're like many people in business, you have a hard time getting your mind clear of the immediate issues on your desk, the activities and decisions that by themselves could chew up a twelve-hour workday. Then there are the institu-tionalized human behaviors that serve as barriers to reality, as we discussed in Chapter 1: filtered information, selective hearing, wishful thinking, fear, emotional overinvestment, and unrealistic expectations of the capital markets. These may not be *your* behaviors, but what about the people you rely on for information? As a leader, you have to wrestle the behaviors of unreality to the ground not only for yourself but also throughout your organization.

Where and how you get your information depends to some degree on the nature of your job. CEOs obviously have a lot of resources to draw on, including direct contact with high-level people outside their own companies, and the resources to hire consultants and advisors. But if you run a business unit, a product line, or profit center, you still have plenty to work with. You have your own contacts in the outside world. The Internet gives you access to ever-increasing amounts of information. And if your need is urgent enough–say, you need to know about a regulatory issue that could affect your business–the CEO should be happy to put you in touch with the people who can help you understand the situation, such as the company's lobby-ist or state or local representatives.

Don't overlook the importance of the media. At a mini-mum, you need to be up to date on what the business jour-nals are covering. Beyond that, the broader your reading, the better able you are to spot drivers of change, patterns, and linkages that aren't always obvious.

Suppose, for example, that you're doing competitor analy-sis. You don't have to hire expensive consultants to learn a lot that can be useful. Companies are always letting the world know what they're doing: product announcements, appointments, plant or office openings and closings, reorganizations. This is useful intelligence if you study it from every conceivable angle, especially the appointments and promotions. Say that Susan Patel is the new general manager of Globeco's Helix division, which hasn't been a thorn in your side in the past. Could she make it into one? She's from marketing. What is she apt to do? What can you find about her past record? You may know somebody who knows somebody who knows her, or you may be able to track down such a person. Post the article or press release on bulletin boards around your organization. Make sure people understand that you're looking for ideas about her.

In the larger environment, you're looking for early warning signals of potentially major change: new entrants in the market, new technologies, regulatory moves. Your ability to weave a pattern out of disparate data and events, separating trends from ephemera and fads, is a key element here.

THE MINDSET OF THE SEEKER

Mostly, though, you need to converse. What could be simpler? Yet we see so many people who don't do it—that is, they don't do it proactively, by asking questions, listening, and keeping their minds open about the answers. This is what good leaders do.

You do it not just in routine meetings but also when you're speaking with people from different parts of the business, or at a trade show, or at lunch with a supplier. You engage others. What are they thinking about? What changes do they see, what opportunities? What worries them? You try to see your business, and the business environment, through the multiple lenses of other people's perception and judgment.

While you're conversing, your mind is unconsciously and automatically processing: "He sees this thing differently than I do. I respect his judgment, so what am I missing?" In the days following you begin to notice things you hadn't seen before. You accumulate more facts, ones that didn't seem important until you had this new perspective. If you finally discover that you need to take an action that hadn't occurred to you before, you've hit the jackpot.

You get information just from walking around with your eyes open. Former Saks Fifth Avenue CEO Arnold Aronson, now a retailing consultant at Kurt Salmon Associates in New York, spends time in stores everywhere he goes, in the evenings and on weekends, from Madison Avenue boutiques to small stores in western Massachusetts. On a vacation to London he made a dazzling discovery in Selfridges, the giant department store. Using restaurants and designer boutiques, the store had segmented its floors for customers of different ages, incomes, and trend consciousness. "We'd been spending decades talking about what it would take to revive the old center-city department stores," he told the *Wall Street Journal.* "Here was a very interesting answer." Aronson's clients across the United States have begun to restructure their own stores accordingly.[2]

One thing you're likely to see today that you didn't see in the past is a CEO wandering the aisles of a store where his product is sold. Procter & Gamble's A. G. Lafley, for example, does this every time he travels. This new breed of CEO looks at product placement and competing products. They talk to store managers about what's selling or not—and why;

they buttonhole customers and ask them what appeals or doesn't. They're focusing on details, but they're also trying to sense structural changes and trends in taste and buying preferences.

In an organization, you sharpen the outside-in view from two different directions. You work down from a broad view of the external environment to your particular circumstances, and at the same time, you work up from your knowledge of the customer and the end user.

■ ■ ■

GE HAS COME UP WITH A MECHANISM that every business leader should consider. One of Jeff Immelt's priorities when he took over as CEO in 2000 was to sharpen the company's view of its external environment. GE was already better than most companies in this regard, but Immelt saw with uncommon clarity that structural changes lay ahead, and that his people would need to spend more time thinking from outside in before making strategic plans.

Immelt's innovation was to divide GE's strategy session into two processes. In the first, each of the company's business units now look only at external changes and issues that seem relevant for the future. Their management teams work up their own ideas and then put their thoughts and questions on a secure website shared by forty to fifty executives representing a cross-section of the multi-industry company. Sharing the multiple perspectives from diverse industries gives everyone new insights and ideas for further discussion and debate.

The business units then gather in GE's Fairfield, Connecticut, headquarters for the first part of the reorganized strategy session, which is devoted solely to discussing external changes, opportunities, and threats—in other words, the external component of a business model. They debate the future of the business. Outsiders with specific expertise in the political and regulatory arenas, global financial systems, technology, and the like are brought in to share their views and answer questions.

For example, suppose GE Aircraft Engines is pondering its future, looking five to twenty years out. The picture is blurred by the poor health of the airline industry, and by the uncertainties surrounding the battle between Boeing and Airbus Industrie. Will more new point-to-point players such as Southwest and JetBlue in the United States, or Ryanair in Europe, arise to challenge the old hub-and-spoke airlines? If so, how might that influence the size of the aircraft? Boeing is losing market share: what's likely to happen to it as a result, and to GE's markets? Will the European Union continue to play a role in underwriting Airbus's development plans? Will the United States do anything that might affect Boeing's health? Will the company ever again be able to take the bold risks in new-plane development it did in the past? What if it continues downhill and Airbus substantially increases its market share? Will Canada's Bombardier and Brazil's Embraer, players in the small-jet marketplace, become more important as regional airlines expand?

The issues and questions surfaced in the session are things managers buried in the day-to-day running of their businesses rarely have time to raise, let alone explore. The give-and-take in the session dialogues create a deeper understanding of business reality, opening up blind spots and surfacing new ideas and insights. The business unit teams leave the session with a wealth of information they can bring back for framing the next step in their planning. When they return to Fairfield later for the planning part of the strategy session, they bring strategic proposals grounded as never before in the realities of the external environment.

In business model terms, Immelt has augmented the iterative thinking that links the three components with an intense exploration of the external component through multiple lenses. The result is a better understanding of not just where the business has been or is, but also of the range of probabilities as to where it is likely to be in the future. Any business unit of any company can bring together knowledgeable people with different points of view about the industry and sort through the complexities to get a clearer understanding of their business environment.

FORGING THE CUSTOMER CHAIN

If you could know all there is to know about your present and potential customer base, including not just their current wants but their future needs, the business environment wouldn't hold too many shocks. You'd be reasonably well prepared for whatever the competitors and other exogenous forces had up their sleeves.

Of all the external information you can gather, knowledge of the customer is the most specific and valuable in assessing your business model or developing new strategies. If this sounds too obvious to be worth stating, then why do so few businesses develop truly intimate understanding of their customers?

Yes, practically everybody claims to focus on the customer, to be customer-centric, or whatever the latest buzzword is. The reality is that most businesses still look at the customer from the inside out, not the other way around. They do their market research (often it's just generic) and then work on things like marketing campaigns, advertising plans, discount programs, and customer service, all focused on delivering an already defined product to the immediate customer. Good service, accurate billing, on-time delivery, no defects, postpurchase support–all these activities are important, but they come after the product or service has been conceived, created, or delivered.

The only way you're going to have differentiation is by knowing people you're hoping to sell to better and sooner than everybody else. If you sell through channels, this means knowing not only the intermediaries but, most important, the ultimate customer–the end user.

You get that knowledge by observing, learning, and thinking about the end user and viewing your own business from the end user's perspective. The starting place for any ideas about what and how to sell must be the final consumer of the product or service. What does he or she really want, need, and place value on? How much is he or she willing to pay?

Think of a supply chain, and then flip the idea around to envision a demand chain or customer chain–a methodology for expanding the extended enterprise into the end user's experience, and focusing on all the elements needed to provide an experience that differentiates your products. To succeed with it, you have to identify the customer's wants and needs much more precisely than before, understand what the customer is willing to pay, and then work backward. Only then can you realistically segment markets, define the combination of attributes the customer prefers, and produce a differentiated customer total experience.

This sequence literally turns the old value chain concept way outside-in, and puts teeth in the idea of customer-centricity. A customer chain is expansive and anticipatory. It's looking at what customers (the people or businesses you sell to) and consumers (the end users of the product or service) need. As companies strive to create discernible differences in their products or services, they must be sure those differences are the ones that really matter to the end user; and because speed counts, that view must be forward looking.

People at all levels of the organization must contribute insights into customers and consumers. Their insights must then be incorporated into the company's decision making, in product development, solutions selling, and the selection and direction of the sales force. Only then can you as a leader realistically shape the company's priorities: where will resources be withheld or spent? Which capabilities need to be developed and which dismantled?

As with the supply chain, the customer chain expands the enterprise outward beyond its four walls. It's critical to build the relationships that allow those insights to surface. What are the pressures, processes, ideas, and opportunities beyond your organization, and how can you work cooperatively with others in the chain between you and the end user to help everyone do better? When your customer's business succeeds, your business does better. This is very different from saying, "I'll sell at this price, and I'll take care of service, quality, and billing." You're trying to find out what other needs the user has.

The clearest way to get a sense of what a customer chain aims to accomplish is to look at small businesses—businesses where the chain is only a single link. Being inherently close to their customers, their proprietors develop intuitive skill bases in understanding customer needs.

■ ■ ■

IN NYACK, NEW YORK, for example, the Herb Lack hardware store prospers year in and year out, despite competition from huge discount stores in nearby malls. Proprietor Lenny Sullivan has seen Pergament come and go, and he's holding off Home Depot and Lowe's. Lenny's prices are higher, of course. His location in a village with a strong commercial base helps, but the real difference is service. Lenny carries a huge array of tools, parts, gadgets, paints, and almost anything you could think of for repairs or a home renovation project. Most important, Lenny and his associates are solution providers. They know how to guide uncertain customers to just the right tool or fitting for their project. They will generate endless paint samples until the color is just the one the customer had in mind. That kind of attention? Priceless.

Then there's Burck Oil in West Palm Beach, Florida. Jeff Burck learned the specialty-lubricants business at a big fuel and lubricants distributor. In 1996 he started his own business. Theoretically, his former employer and other major distributors, with their vast resources and lower prices, had the power to crush him before he even got off the ground. Instead, he has grown steadily larger at their expense. He serves scores of area businesses and most of the local municipalities, selling them lubricants for their police cars, fire engines, maintenance trucks, and heavy equipment. He recently won a big five-year contract from a large fruit producer to supply lubricants for all of its vehicles and machinery.

Jeff's differential advantage is that he takes the time to understand his customers' needs—needs they often don't understand themselves. He analyzes the usage patterns of their equipment, testing their used lubricants to understand which ones are right for the specific conditions of use and which ones aren't. With this information he is able to demonstrate how much the correct lubricant, coupled with ongoing testing, will save them in downtime and replacement costs over time. None of his big competitors offer the same level of attention; indeed, most have cut back on their field staffs in recent years to save money.

This sort of hands-on attention is the central idea behind the "At the Customer, For the Customer" (ACFC) process Jeff Immelt has initiated at GE. "At the customer" can mean that you are literally present with him—an industrial company, for example, might have an office at or near the customer's site. "For the customer" means that you learn her industry, business model, competitiveness, and segmentation, and you help her succeed in multiple ways.

ACFC has changed the way the GE sales force and technical people interact with customers. It is not just another way to wring more sales out of customers, but a program to help customers prosper. GE shows how its technology applications add value to the customer's products, thus enabling the customer to increase market share and improve revenue growth, margins, and cash flow.

Companies such as GE even share their own intellectual capital, such as knowledge of Six Sigma, to help customers improve their productivity. Strengthening their customers' businesses increases their buying power and cements relationships, which in turn generate useful insights. And the close customer contact provides all kinds of hard and soft data, from the understanding of what the customers' new generations of products will be to the social networks behind their decision making.

Successful retailers have been in the forefront of developing customer chains. They are the biggest practitioners of outside-in thinking, because it's both vital to their business models and relatively straightforward compared with the challenge for industrial companies. This is even more so for astute Internet marketers. They know the individual buying habits of their customers based on past sales, and so can target them with specific new offerings as microsegments of one. Amazon.com is the leading exemplar. Using predictive technologies and proprietary algorithms, Amazon can virtually lead a customer by the hand to various stores within its online mall, reasonably confident that it's taking the person to a place he or she would like to explore.

To be sure, it's hard to get everybody in a large business hooked into a customer chain. Organizational structures necessarily divide work into specialized functions such as finance, marketing, engineering, and so on. But what's lost in the division is the integration of diverse information and ideas that take place naturally in a small organization—or in the mind of a proprietor.

Sam Walton recognized the problem, and addressed it with his well-documented market intelligence process—the one where regional managers flew in to Bentonville every week to discuss among themselves and senior managers what was selling or not selling and how Wal-Mart's prices compared with those of local competitors. Everyone learned what products were moving well, what inventory needed to be shifted to where, and what stores or regions were doing better than others. Today this system is fortified at up-to-date retailers with electronic tracking systems that transmit buying patterns instantly to headquarters and to suppliers.

Industrial companies have been slower to develop customer chains, but they're starting to catch on. GE's initiative has its roots in practices developed at such business units as GE Medical Systems, now called GEHealthcare. The unit, which sells high-tech medical equipment to hospitals, was able to tap a huge aftermarket business because of its intimate knowledge of the medical professionals who use its equipment. The sales team spent a lot of time with doctors in the field, talking with and observing them. That close contact allowed them to sort through what doctors really care about. Did radiologists care about resolution, time, or something else? Knowing exactly what the doctor was trying to accomplish with the machinery helped GE Medical focus its research efforts and made new-product introductions far less hit or miss. Its close relationships with doctors also helped it identify a new aspect of the medical industry it could get involved in: information management. This discovery drove a fundamental change in the business, from selling products to selling packages of products and services, and has opened a large new growth trajectory.

Even informal operating mechanisms can contribute to a customer chain. At AlliedSignal in the 1990s, the executive who ran the turbocharger unit put notes from customers on bulletin boards all through the plant and offices. The notes were about things the customers themselves were doing, such as the new products they were developing. The unit also had a section set aside in the plant for each major customer– Bosch, GM, BMW–where its people would come to see their products being made and talk to relevant plant and salespeople.

Learning about end users is harder for companies that sell through intermediaries, and whose ultimate buyer may be several steps down a distribution chain. They generally don't have mechanisms designed to capture information about the customer and end user. They know what the orders and inventory are, but they don't get the immediate feedback about what is moving and what isn't, let alone why.

Information is not always there for the taking, since some distributors don't want their suppliers talking with customers. That's a lose-lose proposition, since the maker of a product is generally better able to interpret and fulfill customer wants than an independent distributor. To be planning a business on the basis of what your industrial distributor wants you to know is just not very wise for either party.

Such distributors might be more cooperative if they understood how megaretailers like Wal-Mart and Home Depot welcome input from their suppliers. They encourage them to take responsibility for their products in the store, to talk with customers, and to use their own imagination to stimulate further sales within their stores.

Getting cooperation with distributors has other benefits to both parties. There may be steps that can be eliminated, cost reductions, or insights into how value is added (or subtracted) along the way. The result can be to make the entire chain not only more cost-competitive but also more effective in delivering value. For example, close cooperation almost always results in reducing the combined inventory of both parties.

Meanwhile, leaders can work on their own to see through the intermediaries. It's much easier for a distributor to heed demands from his customers than from his suppliers. So growing numbers of industrial companies selling through distributors now do what they call customer marketing–conducting their own consumer research so they are not just refilling shelves but analyzing selling patterns to better anticipate customer preferences. They use the information both to guide their own product development and to help retailers understand what will sell best in their stores.

■ ■ ■

WE WANT TO EMPHASIZE that creating a customer chain is not a marketing exercise. It is an essential element of looking around corners, total reorientation of the business to the realities of your customer base, involving all functional areas and organizational levels. Everyone in the business must understand the importance of gathering this kind of information and incorporating it into their everyday decision making.

For most companies, it will be a big change. Even some that have been proficient marketers in the past are not as adept at such marketing activities. You need to be asking the following questions: Does your organization understand its end users? Does it have skills in using that information to identify customer needs and segment the market? Could you create a customer chain next month? If the answer to any of these questions is no, you have your work cut out for you.

Looking around corners is a discipline of its own, and it will be increasingly important in the fast-changing new world of business. Without a strong commitment to understanding where the puck is going to be, and a willingness to make changes based on what you perceive, you risk being overtaken, outcompeted, and obsolete.

CHAPTER 11

Getting Ready

How to Condition Your Culture for Reality

As we saw earlier, Dick Harrington at Thomson, Joe Tucci at EMC, John Chambers at Cisco, Jim McNerney at 3M, and Bob Nardelli at Home Depot took action based on their analysis of what the business model needed and what their organizations could realistically achieve. Operations, people, and organizational processes—known in combination as the corporate culture—often have to change as the business model evolves or gets reinvented. If the company can't make the changes internally, the financial targets get missed, and the business model starts to crumble.

It stands to reason, then, that the more change your organization can handle, the more freedom you have in adjusting your business model. As a leader, you have to be sure your business model is doable, but there's more. You have to make your organization more capable of changing. You have to build in the flexibility you will increasingly need by making your organization change-ready.

Can your company handle the stresses and strains of changes in processes, organization, and even direction or fundamental mission? We've seen countless organizations in which change efforts went awry. The leaders driving the change couldn't give their people the right guidance, and the people couldn't adapt personally or work together to make the changes successful. Why? Because they had no experience with the challenges of significant change.

The navy won't put a ship out to sea until its officers and crew have practiced and drilled their responses to an attack. Your organization needs similar conditioning before sailing into battle. And there's a readily available tool that achieves the same results: the initiative.

An initiative is a specific high-impact project that requires cooperation across the entire organization, such as enterprise resource planning, Six Sigma, or digitization (elimination of paperwork). But it can be much more than a project. Properly designed, led, and executed, an initiative is a lever for cultural change—one that cuts through the intellectual clutter and thumb sucking that so often make culture change a vague, amorphous, and ultimately ineffective undertaking. It's a powerful technique for testing organizational capability and unearthing problems, because it gives you a picture of how people respond to the demands of change in a defined context—a sort of working model of the whole organization's functioning. It focuses everyone on a specific task, to be accomplished to specific standards in a specific time frame. If the initiative runs into trouble, it points out some things you have to improve.

A successful initiative teaches an organization how to unite in action. It helps people face down the fear of failure that keeps so many from trying something new, and gives them the confidence to take on challenges. The benefits are cumulative: the more often you run through the battle stations drill, the better everyone gets at it.

So you start with the dual objectives of identifying the most important projects and building the necessary cooperation and teamwork to support the initiative. The initial projects, once completed, must have high impact so that the organization will gain the confidence and enthusiasm in the value of the effort and embrace a commitment to continue.

Note that we say "properly led." Launching an initiative is one of the most important things a leader can do, requiring his or her total involvement. Nobody to our knowledge has ever tallied the number of initiatives that failed because organizations couldn't handle them, but we would guess the number to be in the hundreds over the past few years.

The usual reason for the failure of an initiative is that it was launched halfheartedly, or was beyond the ability of the organization to master. Here's what tends to happen: The leaders announce a bold new program and then walk away from it, leaving the job to others. With no clear impetus from the top, the program will wander and drift. An initiative, after all, is add-on work, and people already have full plates. Few of them can take it seriously if the boss doesn't. Eventually the effort bogs down and dies.

Leaders also have to make their commitment plain because initiatives often lead to new allocations of resources. There will be winners and losers—a business that's going nowhere, for example, may be told that its cash now has to go to educational efforts necessary to prepare people for the initiatives, such as training everyone in Six Sigma. Without clear direction and help from the top, the would-be losers face the strong and sometimes overwhelming temptation to fight, evade, or sabotage the initiative.

Real results do not come from making bold announcements about how the organization will change. They come from thoughtful, committed leaders who understand the details of an initiative, anticipate its consequences for the organization, make sure their people can achieve it, put their personal weight behind it, and communicate its urgency to everyone.

A successful initiative is a major boost to organizational performance. A failed initiative, by contrast, is a leadership failure with long-term consequences. The damage may not be immediately visible, but it is real and can linger for years. The boss has lost credibility, and the next initiative will be that much harder to launch.

In short, the quality of leadership itself is a critical component of a culture-changing initiative. As we shall see below, the deep personal involvement of the leader in the organization's meetings, councils, and other operations can make an immense difference in a company's performance and competitiveness.

PREPARING THE ORGANIZATION

Initiatives have varying requirements and degrees of difficulty, and it takes a realistic understanding of the organization to make one work. Even a committed leader may misjudge his or her organization—sometimes overestimating its ability and psychological readiness, sometimes underestimating it. A culture that fosters creativity and autonomy above all, for instance, may struggle with initiatives that require consistency across the company. If the pace of change is too fast, the initiative crumbles, leaving the organization dejected or cynical. Yet the pace can also be too slow. When that happens, people don't execute the initiative vigorously, and the business falls behind in its competitive efforts.

When in doubt, start with small steps. Bob Nardelli had the resources to install an inventory replenishment system for Home Depot, which was badly needed to improve inventory turns, but he postponed it because of the corporate culture. He realized that the company's loose entrepreneurial style, one of the keys to its success over the years, would resist a companywide edict from headquarters. Also, the company was not used to formal training programs of any kind, let alone training on information technology. Pushing ahead without a critical mass of store managers able to understand and accept the changes would almost certainly have created chaos. He needed to address the more fundamental need for education, discipline, and accountability first.

The most challenging initiatives like Six Sigma and ERP require a corporate culture in which people are willing to learn new things, understand that delivering on commitments matters, and are comfortable working across boundaries so they can coordinate their efforts and share their experiences. When teamwork, education, accountability, and winning are not valued, it's better to take on a more modest initiative or one better suited to the existing culture and to then build on that success. A company like Home Depot with lots of individuality and entrepreneurship might be successful with an initiative to improve customer service; most store managers could identify closely with the effort.

Succeeding on a small initiative, no matter how simple, provides a foundation for the next. People gain confidence in knowing they can rise to the challenge. That makes it possible to introduce increasingly more difficult and complex initiatives, which people will embrace because they have learned that the struggle will be justified in the end.

■ ■ ■

WHEN I BECAME CEO of AlliedSignal, it was obvious that major changes were in order.* I had lots of ideas about what those changes ought to be. But in my assessment of the existing culture, I saw that the company had no track record of adapting to change. Teamwork was nonexistent, and training and education were geared toward personal improvement rather than practical business problems. I realized that the only way to get the company on track was with a "starter" initiative, one that eased people into the whole process and gave them a taste of success early on.

I started with TQL—total quality leadership, a takeoff on the popular total quality management, which essentially eliminates process steps in manufacturing. It was a simple program, and designed with three objectives in mind: to get people working in teams, to introduce them to problem-solving tools like design of experiments, and to get them to bring to a classroom setting a problem they were having in their work area.

Within a year, the company was ready for the next level, an expansion of TQL's principles into something called TQS—total quality speed. In TQS, teams analyzed various business processes, such as the supply chain and customer satisfaction routine, to identify ways to expedite and improve them. Manufacturing teams, for example, accelerated prod-

---

*This and other sections in this chapter in the first person are coauthor Larry Bossidy's voice.

ucts through various stages of manufacturing. A legal team streamlined AlliedSignal's cumbersome patent application procedures, cutting in half the time it took to get one ready for government approval.

Eighteen months after we launched TQS, teamwork, classroom learning, and practical application of new methodologies had become routine. I felt that Allied was ready for a big one: Six Sigma, the methodological tool-kit for improving all sorts of processes by eliminating variations. I had researched it thoroughly and was convinced that the company badly needed it to reduce defects and variation.

We weren't quite as ready as I'd thought. Many people were skeptical of Six Sigma; they didn't understand the term, and weren't sure they had the capability to master something so technical sounding. It took some urging to get the top ten people to understand it, get their best people to champion it, then devote the necessary resources to education, selecting the projects with the largest impact, and picking the right metrics for measuring improvement. Some leaders took the view that if they just kept their heads down, this too would pass. Some of them had to be reassigned. Nevertheless, our quality was measurably rising after six months. Within a year the changes were dramatic, improving our revenues on one hand and cost and inventory turns on the other. In addition, we were able to extend this effort to our customers and suppliers. We moved on to ERP and digitization, benefiting in both from the established discipline of Six Sigma (ERP in particular, with its inflexible model, requires intense discipline for success).

After AlliedSignal's merger with Honeywell in 1999,

momentum waned, partly because of the long uncertainty around the proposed merger with GE that never came to pass. When I returned from retirement in 2001 to get the company back on track and select a successor, we immediately launched a companywide digitization initiative. The idea behind this effort was to use information technology to eliminate paper, and save money—a target of $500 million in three years. Dave Cote, my successor, continued driving this initiative and in the fall of 2003 he was able to report that the company had hit its savings target just twenty-two months into the initiative, more than a year ahead of schedule. He has now effectively launched "Design for Six Sigma" and a growth initiative.

You don't have to map out a series of initiatives ahead of time. At AlliedSignal and Honeywell we just kept in tune with the external and internal realities. Our choice of initiatives was always guided by the need to stay ahead of and close the gap with the competition, but the pace was tempered by what the organization could absorb. As soon as one initiative took hold, we moved on to the next thing that had to be done.

WHAT'S THE RIGHT INITIATIVE FOR YOUR ORGANIZATION?

In the new environment, with its ever-intensifying battles for razor-thin advantages, almost any edge you can gain looks attractive. And the list of tools and methodologies an organization can use to improve is endless. These days the most popular initiatives are moving operations to low-cost regions, streamlining the supply chain, and Six Sigma. These initiatives are being widely adopted because they aim squarely at the challenges so many companies face: reducing cost and improving productivity and quality.

Other initiatives range from a variety of process improvements to analytical tools such as the balanced scorecard, which augments traditional financial measures with criteria for such things as customer satisfaction and business process effectiveness. Companies continue to devote considerable time to integrating information technology functions through such programs as ERP and the acquisition of facilitating software.

Keeping in mind that you're as interested in conditioning your organization for dealing with change as you are in achieving specific improvements, we see a number of additional noteworthy initiatives coming down the road.

One is achieving uniform IT technology and software. Far too much money is being lost as companies try to cobble together different systems. Unifying them leads to enormous savings and productivity improvements. You might think this is strictly an IT issue, rather than a driver of broad cultural adaptation, but it isn't. It takes enormous cooperation across the business for people to give up their familiar software and adapt to new systems. The same is true for adapting to outsourced computing power versus owning your own machines—something more companies are doing in order to increase flexibility and lower capital needs.

Another is keeping talent within the organization. Anything you can do to create more job freedom will yield real gains in morale and performance. The workplace keeps getting more demanding as companies ratchet up productivity, and leaders need to give more time and attention to mitigating the burdens. For example, managers need to be more creative in helping people find ways to divide work between office and home. This is particularly important for those with young children.

Indeed, an enormous amount of talent is being wasted because many women are forced to drop out when they have children. What can you do to keep them aboard? One technique might be to help groups organize themselves as contract companies that work as a variant of a temp agency. Two or more women, each working part time, could share a full-time job and provide the continuity that an employer needs.

■ ■ ■

PEOPLE CAN BE MORE productive in the workplace if they have better control of their free time. One approach is to give them their time off in different increments. Working, say, ten days and taking four off doesn't change the ratio of working to nonworking days, but for many people a four-day break would be much more desirable than the customary weekends.

What's important is to pick the initiative that's right for your business. A lot of corporate energy is expended on initiatives and "improvements" because they're the formula du jour–the latest fad or buzz-concept. We're talking not just about the obvious misfires (remember quality circles and zero defects?) but about anything that's suddenly popular that may not necessarily be a top priority given your circumstances at the moment. "I saw a company with a great supply chain," a leader will say. "Let's put that in." Or, "We have to do Six Sigma because everybody else is." Often as not, the organizational energy and resources end up being wasted. When the next initiative comes along, people groan and say, "Here we go again."

The improvements you choose must be guided by the priorities in your business model. The critical areas are the operating strengths and weaknesses that affect the business's ability to generate cash earnings over time–things like cost, productivity, profitable revenue growth, differentiation, speed, and quality. For example, if you need to raise cash flow, look to such things as improving inventory turns or a process improvement that speeds the collection of receivables.

Whatever the choice, always be sure the initiative is something your people can handle. Remember that you're not only aiming for a specific improvement but also training the organization for adaptation and trying to build unity and alignment. If it takes an easy or uncomplicated task to get people ready, suppress your impatience and make sure you lay the groundwork.

We have seen operating initiatives designed with these criteria in mind literally save companies. In 1989, Emmanuel ("Mano") Kampouris was named CEO of American Standard. American Standard, then a $3.6 billion diversified manufacturer known best for plumbing products, had become heavily leveraged as the result of a management-led buyout undertaken to ward off a hostile takeover by Black & Decker. That left the company with a business model where cash was king: the company desperately needed to generate lots of it to preserve liquidity and reduce debt.

Kampouris's backers and lenders advised him to do what seemed obvious: sell off some businesses, use the proceeds to pay down debt, and focus on improving margins in the remaining businesses. But Kampouris, a seasoned and business-savvy leader, believed he could meet the model's thirst for cash and still keep American Standard largely intact. Most of the businesses earmarked for divestiture had strong markets and growth prospects; they just happened not to be generating enough cash, given the new debt load. If he could improve margins and asset utilization in those and the other businesses, they would produce enough cash not only to service the debt but also to position American Standard for growth. As the company improved its cash-generating ability, it could do an equity issue, further reduce the debt, and become bigger and stronger than ever.

Kampouris set out to improve the components of the business model, radically altering manufacturing flow, inventory management, and management of accounts receivable. Comfortable in international business settings, and a keen observer and listener, he literally traveled the world in search of tools and techniques that would help his company. He picked up a lot of ideas along the way. But he hit the jackpot at home when he met John Costanza, an information technology consultant in Colorado.

Costanza was developing something he called demand flow manufacturing (DFM), a system that aligned people, machines, and materials for the most efficient possible workflow. It was a system 180 degrees opposite to what every plant manager and operations manager had been taught, one that underlies the concept of "lean manufacturing." Working with Costanza, Kampouris personally mastered the concepts and details, drew in his senior management team, and then decreed that every manager be trained in it. The result was nothing less than total victory. American Standard's annual inventory turns almost tripled between 1989 and 1996, generating some $460 million in cash annually. The company held on to all the desired businesses in its portfolio and still was able to reduce its debt ahead of time. Its equity offering was a smashing success.

HOW TO LEAD AN INITIATIVE

There are no free throws with initiatives: if one is important enough to launch, it cannot be allowed to fail. Failure costs time and money and, more important, affects the whole psyche of the organization. When a new program is launched and then fizzles, people lose their energy and enthusiasm; it won't be easy to charge them up the next time around. Meanwhile, competitors have plenty of opportunities to outmaneuver the distracted and anxious troops. For some companies, the initiative is the last chance at becoming adaptable and financially viable.

This is where leadership gets very personal. The leader's follow-through is what keeps the initiative alive and encodes it into the organization's DNA. Kickoff speeches and delegation are not enough. Leading an initiative requires intense focus, hard work, tremendous time, and endless physical and emotional energy. Before you start down the path, ask yourself: Do you understand the initiative well enough to develop metrics to evaluate how the implementation is going? Are you willing to commit the necessary resources for education? Do you have the focus and discipline to drive it through the organization? Do you have the stamina to repeatedly convey the importance of the initiative through your actions as well as your words? Do you have the courage to confront those who are standing in the way? Is cynicism changing to excitement?

The more ambitious the initiative, the more deeply involved you have to be. Six Sigma, for example, can make a huge difference in an organization's productivity; it has generated dazzling results at GE, Honeywell, and 3M, among other places, but only because the leaders led. It's applicable not only in manufacturing but in everything from marketing to human resources. It takes discipline and commitment to make it work, and we have seen all too many attempts that failed because the leaders didn't do their jobs. One of the most poignant examples is Motorola. Founder and chairman Bob Galvin was a successful pioneer of Six Sigma in the late eighties and early nineties. But after Galvin retired, none of his successors picked up the baton with the same enthusiasm, and the company's performance suffered as a result.

There are four imperatives for the leader launching an initiative: learn the guts of it, invest your time and energy, pick the right people to initiate it, and be courageous.

Learn the Guts of the Initiative The leader has to really dig into whatever approach or technique the organization is taking on. That doesn't mean writing a textbook on it, but it does mean taking the time to master the basic principles, as Mano Kampouris did. No shortcuts, no excuses, even if the details are boring or technical.

■ ■ ■

WHEN I FIRST GOT INTERESTED in Six Sigma, I wanted to be sure I really understood it before I made any decisions or took any actions, so I got help from an expert who had lots of practical experience implementing it at Motorola and ABB, the global provider of power and automation technologies. I didn't learn all of the statistical aspects of it as a Six Sigma "black belt" would, but I learned the methodology and the tools. Because I mastered the guts of it, I was completely comfortable fielding questions about it and responding to people's concerns in front of any audience. My business experience had taught me how to link the outcome of the applications of this tool to margin, cost, cash, and growth.

My knowledge helped me to judge whether Six Sigma was really taking root. When I'd ask someone how it was going in his part of the business, I could tell just from how he answered my questions whether he was genuinely involved or had passed the implementation off to others. I could recognize who was passing the buck, making excuses, refusing to change, or otherwise getting in the way of progress. In other words, my understanding helped reduce the snow factor.

Mano Kampouris could teach demand flow manufacturing for six hours without notes. When he stepped onto the factory floor at one of the divisions, he could tell almost immediately whether DFM was being used effectively. And when people reported back that they were running into trouble at their plant, he could gauge where the problem was. Did the division manager really understand DFM? Was he or she teaching the plant people? Or was there some legitimate glitch? Kampouris's knowledge made it nearly impossible for others to bluff, and he linked rewards for all officers to certification in the process. When some leaders consistently failed to deliver, he knew they were unwilling to change their ways, and he replaced them rather than see the initiative thwarted.

Key members of the business team also should learn the guts of the initiative. If leaders throughout the company don't grasp the initiative or buy in to it, the implementation is likely to go bust. All the leaders we know who've made Six Sigma work insisted that their direct reports receive the same intense training in Six Sigma that they did.

Invest Your Time and Energy in the Initiative Knowledge of the initiative can help a leader decide whether to take it on, but once that decision gets made, there's no turning back. He or she must make a personal commitment to spend the tremendous amount of time and energy required to keep the organization focused. The time commitment alone explains why companies must be selective about which, and how many, initiatives to tackle. As Kampouris recognized, major initiatives require changes in the metrics of how managers are measured. Regular reviews and follow-through are the sine qua non for getting the initiative to move forward and cut through resistance.

People throughout an organization watch the leader's every move, so he or she must be mindful of the messages that come through in actions as well as words. Behavior—everything from what gets talked about how often to body language—must reinforce the same consistent message.

■ ■ ■

DURING THE FIRST YEAR of Six Sigma at AlliedSignal I spent a good 20 percent of my time talking to all the classes in which people were being prepared for Six Sigma, traveling to Europe to speak at celebratory dinners honoring those who had completed their black-belt training, and the like. Later, when Honeywell adopted Six Sigma, I began every meeting with the business units and every performance review by discussing how the Six Sigma effort was going. Which people had been trained? Which projects did they tackle? How did those projects link to the business model? Obviously, the executives would be embarrassed if they couldn't answer those questions or if the answers somehow showed that the initiative was on the back burner. If their CEO wasn't losing interest in the initiative, neither could they.

■　■　■

SOME LEADERS MAKE IT ALL TOO CLEAR that they aren't deeply committed. One executive we know actually dozed off during a progress report on a major corporate initiative. The message came through loud and clear to his team: if this stuff is so darn boring, is it really necessary? No wonder the initiative never amounted to much in that company. Another delivered a speech that was direct and businesslike but completely devoid of emotion, providing no evidence of personal commitment. Leaders can't afford to have bad days in public settings.

Major initiatives tap your emotional reserves, but you must be tireless. Conviction and excitement must come through in every speech and conversation. Repetition and even exaggeration are necessary tools; so is the occasional burst of fire-and-brimstone. You have to assert, declare, and continually reinforce the fact that the initiative is not just a test or an experiment but is vital to the company's competitiveness and therefore is here to stay. Jack Welch admitted to exaggerating the importance of Six Sigma just to be sure it was getting through to people, and it did, even in parts of the organization where it was a harder sell. I talked about Six

Sigma with such frequency that I'm sure some of the people in the audience were thinking they finally had located the "one-watt bulb" and he was standing before them.

Pick the Right People to Implement the Initiative Naturally you want people who are enthusiastic about leading initiatives, but you also need to make sure they're functionally suited to the job and motivated to make things happen. Let's say you plan an initiative to improve the supply chain. Make it a special reporting job with specific performance metrics, and put someone without a conflict of interest in charge—that is, assign a person who understands manufacturing but is not currently working in it. However competent and conscientious the manufacturing folks might be, their immediate concerns often run counter to the broader agenda of the supply chain. Because they typically want to make everything internally, they're hard-pressed to evaluate outsourcing opportunities appropriately. Or if you're setting up an operation overseas, be sure that the people assigned to address the issue have the right mentality and cultural awareness to undertake the task. For example, we often see American managers who either condescend to professionals in other countries or act as all-knowing drill instructors. Such behavior can do a lot of damage; leaders have to keep an eye out for it, and take whatever remedial action is necessary.

Be Courageous Since important initiatives are likely to significantly change the way many people operate, they can pose a major test of your strength and determination. Some people will scream; some will drag their heels; some will even try to quietly sabotage the effort.

Changing the organizational structure will create real or perceived winners and losers. Reallocating resources requires dealing with the aggrieved constituencies and making sure that good people aren't discouraged or driven out when their part of the business is cut down. Outsourcing jobs might mean severing employees who've served loyally and well. Important initiatives often require pulling the very best people off other projects where their absence will be felt.

Leaders must have the courage of their convictions to follow through, and they have to be both inspiring and unrelenting. People need to know that there will be consequences for not getting behind the initiative. The message has to be "We've thought about the pros and cons and concluded that this is something we must do. Therefore it is a high priority, and we've laid out the steps. If people aren't on board with us, there will have to be changes made."

■ ■ ■

CHANGES IN REWARDS CAN ADD MUSCLE to the message. I made some very valuable managers unhappy during the early years of Six Sigma because others who were involved in the initiative got better rewards and recognition. But that was the point: I wanted leaders to think hard about the benefits of becoming black belts in Six Sigma.

At AlliedSignal, and later at Honeywell, each year we graphed how many people were trained in Six Sigma, how many people were promoted out of the program, and the ratings of the people they picked. At its early stages, some

30 percent of a business unit leader's bonus was tied to progress on Six Sigma.

I also used visibility to create accountability. As soon as I had the plan ready to launch, I told my team that they were going with me to present it to the security analysts. "But we don't know how to do this yet," some complained. "That's okay, you're coming with me," I said. "If I fail, we all fail, and it will be in public." There was no ambiguity about the group's responsibility for the success of the initiative.

A successful initiative is a great legacy for the future: when successive leaders keep the faith, companies gain strength as each person brings something new to the table. In 2000, Fred Poses, formerly vice chairman at AlliedSignal, succeeded Mano Kampouris at American Standard. He found a sound business model and a nice system for achieving asset turnover and cash generation. Demand flow management was alive and well. It also was not enough. Productivity improvement hadn't reached beyond the factory, and new products were too slow getting to market. While continuing to drive DFM, Fred moved ahead with other initiatives. Building on Mano's solid foundation, he took American Standard to the next level. Its stock has risen 250 percent since he took over.

My successor at Honeywell, Dave Cote, has already established two new initiatives, one Design for Six Sigma, the other relating to growth.

CHAPTER 12

Leading for Reality

Early in Bob's career he'd been marked as a high-potential candidate for senior management, maybe even the top job. Each succeeding assignment confirmed that he was indeed an outstanding leader. A can-do guy, he made ambitious commitments and kept them. He was clearheaded, self-aware, a good listener, and tough but fair; every team he assembled loved working with him. His integrity was rock solid.

In 1999 Bob was made the CEO of his $3 billion company. Four years later he took early retirement "for personal reasons." The board expressed its deep regret in a glowing letter, but everyone in the company knew that Bob had basically been fired.

What on earth happened to Bob? Answer: The new business environment. Two years after he took the helm, the company's premier division, accounting for more than half of its revenues, began to find its prices under severe pressure. Bob knew the division well, since he'd spent much of his career in it. He'd faced such difficulties before, and he was confident that the division's management team could rise to the challenge. He'd put the team together, after all, and they knew just about everything he knew. He agreed with their proposed responses: tighten costs further, start the long-planned supply chain initiative, and get marketing to rethink its programs. The team executed their plans quickly, but the competitor still kept gaining ground.

After a board meeting, one of the directors pulled Bob aside and quietly suggested that maybe he needed to do something more drastic. Bob listened, in his characteristic studious way, but the director wasn't very specific, and Bob couldn't imagine what such a thing might be. Anyway, he concluded, the competitor could not afford to keep fighting this price war much longer.

The competitor, as it happened, had been qualified by Wal-Mart in 2000. This didn't worry Bob much, since his division's products were mostly sold in upscale and specialty stores. What Bob didn't know was that Wal-Mart's demanding criteria for its suppliers had driven the competitor to a new level of efficiency and speed. It had outsourced some production to eastern Europe and tightened its own supply chain; it had adjusted its business model to the lower cost structure, and was able to drop prices significantly while maintaining its margins. What's more—and this was one of the things Bob couldn't imagine—it had become thoroughly customer-centric. It had learned how to work closely with the retailers it served in understanding changing patterns of customer needs.

The competitor migrated what it had learned over to its higher-value lines—the ones that competed with Bob's division—and pressed its advantages aggressively. By the time Bob's division responded, the competitor's momentum was unstoppable. At the end of 2003 Bob's division was a wreck.

Its market share had declined by half, its margins had shrunk to the thinness of tissue paper, and it had become a drain on corporate resources.

The critical change Bob missed was this: Previously the competitor and Bob's division had the same business model. But the competitor had changed its model. What it learned about operations from Wal-Mart and applied to the third component (strategy, operations, people, and organization) recalibrated the financial targets of the middle component. The new model made Bob's model obsolete.

Bob met all the traditional criteria of leadership, but he didn't have the qualities needed in today's business environment. He didn't have a realistic view of the external environment; his information came from like-minded people in the organization. He'd maintained a good business and grown it, but he hadn't faced the need for drastic change before, and hadn't ever taken risks. He knew how to respond to a familiar, straight-ahead competitive challenge, but not to a change serious enough to affect his business model, coming from a wholly unexpected direction. When trouble hit, he did the only things he knew how to do. He did them well—Bob always did what he did well—but they weren't adequate for the new challenge.

Companies are full of people like Bob: talented, hardworking men and women whose time-honored leadership qualities have taken them to the top of a business but nevertheless aren't adequate for the task now at hand. We must be brutally blunt about this: only the leaders who have the capacity to recognize reality for what it is have a good chance to succeed in the new environment. Those who can't should rethink their career plans before the decisions are made for them.

THE NEW LEADERSHIP CRITERIA

The fact is that any business expecting to stay around in the new environment has to raise the bar for leadership. Some qualities will always be essential—things like discipline, integrity, maturity, and ego containment. But a number of deficiencies that were tolerable in the past, such as the inability to hear new points of view, are no longer so. Several qualities that often got short shrift in the selection of leaders are now high on the list of leadership criteria, and we'll talk about these momentarily.

Two leadership qualities have become absolutely indispensable today, and they aren't on the usual lists. The first is business acumen, more commonly called business savvy. The second is a need to know—or, to put it another way, a refusal to take anything for granted, and insatiable curiosity about what's new and different.

Business Savvy In the most recent of his annual letters to Berkshire Hathaway shareholders—letters widely admired for their common sense and candor—Warren Buffet referred to an executive he'd put in charge of a newly acquired business as a man with business savvy. Buffet, whose own business savvy is legendary, felt no need to explain what he meant, and we suppose that most of his readers felt that they understood what he was saying.

Yet like the business model, the meaning of the phrase is

often in the ear of the beholder. Significantly, we've never seen it defined in any standard lists of leadership traits, the sort compiled by academics and human resource executives. So just what do we mean by business savvy?

People with business savvy understand how to make money. In effect, as discussed in Chapter 5, they have business models in their minds: they understand all three components of the model and their relationships. They have a gut feel for the external environment that enables them to identify patterns and trends likely to affect their businesses. They understand the strengths and weaknesses of their business's internal activities. They search constantly for the mix of financial targets that will be consistent both with each other and with the model's other components. They are driven to solve problems and identify opportunities. At the end of the day, they measure their success not by the power they've wielded or the praise they've won, but by the satisfaction of knowing that they've met their financial targets.

People with business savvy also know that a fundamental simplicity underlies all of these details. When they've sorted and weighed the complexities and variables, they know what can and can't be known; they know what's concrete and what's ambiguous. In doing this, they have found simplicity and achieved clarity. And like outstanding teachers, they can then convey this simple understanding to those they work with.

If there's a downside to business savvy, it's that people who have it tend to rely on their gut instincts. As a result they generally don't feel the need to do deep research to support their views and decisions. This leads us to . . .

The Need to Know We confess to a longstanding fondness for the title former Intel CEO Andy Grove put on his book: *Only The Paranoid Survive.* We don't advocate paranoia, but Grove had a point: something close to paranoia is essential for survival in this environment. Call it a permanently heightened state of alert, a kind of running "code orange," an understanding that you almost never have all the pieces of the puzzle, or—as it's called in India—"divine discontent." Something out there somewhere could affect your business, now or in the future, and you can't be satisfied until you find out what it is.

The need to know is a relentless quest for the critical one percent of information that can make all the difference to your business prospects. It's the desire to see to the horizon and, to the extent possible, what might lie beyond. Leaders with this quality alternately look down the road to see what's ahead and over their shoulder to see who might be coming up from behind. They are far less likely to be blindsided than those who don't, and far more likely to be in control of their business's destiny.

Business savvy has always been a quality in short supply; it's considered more or less inherent, and not many people are born with it. But any leader who can learn how to use the business model will acquire the essential elements of business savvy. Those who also cultivate the attitudes and aptitudes of needing to know will be fully equipped to confront reality, and well on their way to being complete businesspeople. Together, these qualities give you the power to see the world as it is, not as you wish it to be, and to do what needs to be done, not what you necessarily would like to do.

We mentioned that several traditional leadership qualities are more critical now than before. These include intellectual honesty, comfort with ambiguity, self-confidence, and courage. But if you have business savvy and the need to know, you're a good bet to have these other qualities as well: they come with the territory.

Your grasp of the fundamentals of making money will help to keep you intellectually honest. Your pursuit of knowledge will condition you to accept the ambiguity of that which can't be completely known. You'll have the self-confidence to make the tough judgment calls. This is not the confidence that is puffed up by an enlarged view of the self, but the true confidence that comes naturally with business savvy: an assurance generated by the knowledge that you're in touch with the external and internal realities and their relationships. And you'll have the true courage to take whatever actions are necessary to increase the intrinsic value of your business, no matter how difficult or even contrarian they may be.

Some leaders who've piled success on top of success as they climbed the corporate ladder fail when the reach the top because they don't have these qualities. We've seen it happen to people we know, like, and have worked with– good leaders with stellar records, like Bob. And we've seen it happen with increasing frequency in recent years.

Take the case of James, a young business unit leader we know whose boss had set ambitious growth targets for 2003. The second quarter had scarcely started when he began to realize that the goal would be unreachable because the division's customers were suffering in the face of new foreign competition.

Realistically, James should have gone to his boss and explained the situation: this was not a short-term problem but a structural change. Instead he soldiered on in an increasingly hopeless cause. Why? There were two reasons. First, he'd built his reputation on his ability to grow his business under difficult circumstances, and he didn't want to jeopardize it by letting his boss down. Second, he knew he couldn't just say, "This won't work," and let it go at that. In laying out the realities to his boss, he'd have to present one or more alternative options for the unit. But he couldn't come up with any that made sense. James knew one thing well, and that was how to grow a business, but that's all he knew. And he didn't have the intellectual integrity to confront his reality and deal with it. His failure let down his whole team and damaged his career badly.

Many leaders like Bob and James came up on the fast track, selected and groomed on the basis of leadership criteria that, realistically speaking, have declining value. These are the personality traits often highly prized by headhunters and other evaluators of people. They advance because they're articulate. They have good presentation skills and communicate well. They have (to use a word headhunters love) "heft"—meaning the energy and forcefulness to bull their way through opposition and prevail. They've got vision, perseverance, the ability to motivate and inspire, and good track records.

Such people are usually indeed talented and hardworking. They just may not have what it takes for leadership today. They've advanced on the basis of their past performance but haven't been tested for their business savvy or their ability to anticipate and deal with new and disruptive business conditions. Companies won't fully succeed in confronting reality until they make a priority of revising their leadership criteria.

Businesses also need to find ways to reward leaders who *do*

confront reality. Many compensation plans, designed to encourage long-term thinking, include an incentive based on a
three-year period of earnings or revenue growth. But what
happens when the leader discovers at the end of the second
year that some radical and costly changes are called for? How
many leaders would willingly interrupt earnings and put their
own and everyone else's bonus at risk? More likely, the leader
will defer the moves for another year. If the business has a lot
of cash and little debt, leaders can defer the inevitable for
years. There's got to be a way to reward a leader who says, "I
see a storm coming, and we have to do something that's a big
departure from our plan." The focus must be on getting ahead
of the crisis, and always on building intrinsic value. Leaders
must be rewarded for running the business in a way that will
sustain it.

PRACTICING THE NEED TO KNOW

Chapter 10 explained the many ways of looking around
corners for the threats and opportunities that come with increasing speed and frequency in the new business environment. But none of these techniques will amount to much in
an organization whose leaders aren't attitudinally driven by
the need to know. Too often, leaders are wrapped up in what
goes on inside the walls of their companies.

Those who anticipate trouble and opportunity, we have
observed, are always looking for new information—ideas,
viewpoints, theories, scenarios. They want to hear what customers, suppliers, and people outside their own industries
think. They know that they can never know enough; that
they can't rely on past assumptions as guides to the present

and future. They seek diverse sources of information, and listen more than they talk. They scrutinize all the components of the business model, from the external scan and root-cause analysis to the robustness of the financial targets to the capabilities of the organization itself. The result: they see reality more clearly than others. They don't have to cling to the status quo for security.

Leaders who drive for reality don't shoot the messengers who bring bad news. Whether it's an outside source with a new piece of reality or a team leader in a meeting who says, "This project is heading for trouble," they listen attentively. Indeed, they encourage people to challenge received wisdom. They constantly ask questions: What could go wrong to blow this strategy out of the water? What will happen if the Chinese revalue the yuan? Is this new technology I read about a threat to the product we're developing? They weigh the new information they get with intellectual honesty, and take whatever actions are required because of it.

It's not just trouble they look for, but opportunities as well. For example the rising hue and cry over rising health-care costs has an implicit hopelessness to it. Nothing can be done, it seems, to stop this trend. But leaders in all sorts of business think otherwise, and are making money with their ideas. GE Health systems created a new health-care information management product line, which among other things is helping hospitals digitize their operations. The age of antiterrorism has created opportunities for companies making security systems, sensors, signal processing equipment, and the like, ranging from companies such as IBM and Honeywell to defense contractors like Lockheed Martin.

Outsourcing, which worries many in the developed economies, will yield opportunities in the immense markets of China and India. For example, Procter & Gamble and Colgate have extensive outsourcing relationships in these countries, but more than that they are getting to know potential customers—even in rural areas—and designing products specifically tailored to their income levels. They recognize that if they can sell profitably to these still-poor consumers now, the brand loyalty will pay off big time as developing countries' incomes rise and their currencies are revalued.

Leaders who pay attention to all of the information, signs, and portents don't have to lean on conventional wisdom, which is often apt to thwart the very actions that could make the difference between success and failure. Recall the story of Lou Gerstner at IBM: his willingness to buck conventional wisdom was what he called "the single most important decision of my career," and it saved IBM.[1]

Conventional wisdom is what you get when you rely on past solutions and listen to like-minded people, and it's one of the greatest challenges to realistic thinking. On the one hand, these are people whose experience and judgment you've learned to value, and you naturally respect what they have to say. On the other hand, it's hard for like-minded people to dispute the collective judgment with viewpoints that originate outside the club—viewpoints that could change the equation dramatically.

For leaders who recognize that a new reality is taking shape in real time, the past is only a prelude to what they need to do next. They devote their intellectual and emotional energies not to politicking and furtherance of ambition but to broadening their understanding. They visualize scenarios—opportunities and threats—like movies in their brains; they dream, and they conceptualize.

■ ■ ■

IN 2002, DURING MY LAST MONTHS as chairman and CEO of Honeywell, I had narrowed my search for a successor to two well-qualified finalists, both of whom were from outside the company.* One was the former COO of a large industrial company, and the other was Dave Cote, CEO of TRW.

On the strength of their résumés, I might have picked the first candidate. He had a great breadth of experience in diverse industries, and had earned a reputation for outstanding performance. Dave also had a solid track record, but was less seasoned.

After checking as many references as possible, I sat down with each man for the final interview. The first candidate was all that his résumé claimed, and he was bright and personable. But during the nearly four hours of conversation, all he talked about were the things he'd done in his career, his many challenges and accomplishments. He had practically nothing to say about the future of those businesses, or about the changing business environment and what it might mean for his next assignment. He didn't exhibit any sign of the need to know.

Dave turned out to have a natural inclination to look ahead. He wanted to know what was changing in Honeywell's extended industry and customer base, and what those

*This section and other parts of this chapter in the first person are by coauthor Larry Bossidy.

things would mean in terms of future profitability. He asked questions such as "What market segments remain untapped? How much can the people grow from these jobs? What do the customers think about your products?" It was clear that he was curious and a learner; he'd grown, and, most important, would continue to grow. It was also clear he was eager for action—that he wanted to not just maintain what I had done but to do whatever different was necessary to take Honeywell to the next level. When he left the interview, my recommendation to the board was an easy one.

FINDING CLARITY IN COMPLEXITY

The best information isn't much use if you can't make sense of it. While running a business has never been simple, the internal and external issues that face leaders today are more numerous, complex, and interrelated than ever before. Many leaders have vast amounts of knowledge and are bursting with ideas but lack the ability to sort through complicated issues with many variables, identify the underlying realities, and distinguish the root causes from the symptoms.

Pricing problems, for example, are often a tip-off on deeper problems the leader has to understand. When a customer is not willing to pay your price, it's time to dig into the underlying conditions. Somebody must have lower costs, or a better product. It can't be brushed off with comments like "Everyone is having pricing problems." For example, a person with business savvy knows that improving productivity, while important, does not necessarily increase margins. The pricing behavior of competitors and customers' needs for the product mix are important determinants of margins.

■ ■ ■

About three or four years ago, the leaders in Honeywell's plastic business saw a decline in profit and revenue, which then began to affect margins. I met with them to find out why this was happening and what they planned to do about it. They answered the second question—they would cut costs to bolster the margins. But they didn't answer the first question, which was the fundamental one. Cutting costs might help for only a year or two: without knowing the root cause of the decline, they couldn't know whether they could continue to make money in the longer term.

So I grilled them. The competition had lowered its prices: Why? How deep was the price differential? Was there a product difference? Were they going offshore? Was there excess capacity, and if so, who was creating it? Would it be likely to shrink, or would it be around for a long time? Asked to confront the reality of the situation, they were forthcoming. The management team acknowledged that the product was being priced as a commodity, and that we did not have the scale to compete on cost or price. Their honesty and knowledge of the situation culminated in a decision to exit the business.

And it was an important lesson for the management team. They learned that they had to get to the root cause of a problem if they were going to do anything more than put a temporary patch on it.

■ ■ ■

The ability to find clarity in complexity is critical in creating a robust business model. You and your team have to be able to sort through the model's components in their many combinations, drill diagnostically to determine which parts are working and which aren't, and make a sound judgment about which combination will get results given the current realities.

THE COURAGE TO CHANGE

We see many leaders with the intelligence to recognize that they've reached a crossroad but who don't follow through and head down the new path. Their inner core isn't tough enough to allow them to acknowledge and deal with an unpleasant reality, whether it's closing a plant or abandoning an established way of doing business. They may want to stay in the comfort zone of their familiar managerial routines. They may be protecting their paychecks. They may be afraid: change means taking overt risks, and taking risks raises the possibility of failure.

These leaders often don't recognize that failing to make a shift can be riskier than making one; or that it may deprive them of an opportunity to do something great, as Thomson Corp. did. Even more pathetic are the ones who understand this but would rather risk a quiet failure of the status quo than one illuminated by the spotlight of a change agenda.

The leaders who have the stomach for tough action have inner strength. They are willing to look clearly at the business environment and if necessary accept that the business model that has been highly successful—the model the leader may even have built her career on—is no longer relevant. They are willing to tackle the intricacies of the business model, make judgments about what will and won't work, and make the painful decisions that follow from changing it. These leaders do not just adapt: they visualize the probabilities and then move to take advantage of them. They know there's risk involved. But like EMC's Joe Tucci, they have learned that in this environment, a business may have to disrupt itself before someone else does the disrupting.

You don't usually find leaders with this kind of toughness adorning themselves with brashness, boldness, and big public personalities. The kind of courage we're talking about plays out in the accuracy of the leader's perceptions, her clarity of judgment, and her willingness to make unpopular moves for the sake of building a viable business that is in tune with reality.

During his first two years as GE's CEO, Jeff Immelt took realistic short-term action to build for the long term. His moves slowed the relentless pace of earnings per share growth investors had enjoyed for two decades. Yet Immelt is widely admired, and in fact the *Financial Times* named him its Man of the Year for 2003. Why? In part because he took the lead in governance reform, but largely because he had the courage to say that the enterprise he inherited needed to be retooled for a new business environment and was willing to endure the short-term consequences.

Immelt had coincidentally arrived just as the business world was undergoing its radical changes. Taking a long and disciplined look at GE's external environment—or what he calls its "context"—he recognized that GE's business model itself needed retooling. Among other things, he concluded that the greatest growth opportunities would lie in the world's developing economies, notably China and India, and that technology, services, and intensive focus on the customer would be essential elements of growth businesses.

At a two-day offsite meeting in the summer of 2003, Immelt presented a detailed analysis of GE's external context, linking it with his foresight about the future possibilities of GE businesses. His insights gave the board members a clear framework for discussing and approving major strategic decisions, such as subsequent opportunities in health care and the acquisition of the Vivendi Universal entertainment businesses.

The centerpiece of the new model was a set of explicit five-year financial targets: revenue growth at least twice the rate of U.S. GDP growth; a return on equity of better than 20 percent; and growth in cash generation of ten percent a year. He also aimed for a triple A balance sheet (which only a handful of companies listed on the New York Stock Exchange can boast); and stock price appreciation equal to or better than the S&P 500 average.

Meeting those targets has forced changes in every part of the model's third component, internal activities. Strategically, Immelt refocused the company on global markets where it can achieve long-range growth trajectories. His six growth platforms include health-care information technology, water technology and services, oil and gas technology, security and sensors, Hispanic media, and U.S. consumer finance. All of these are linked to what Immelt calls "unstoppable trends" in the global economy.

He is shedding some traditional businesses, such as part of the insurance business, and putting others on the block. And he's invested heavily (some $30 billion in 2003 alone) in acquisitions to augment others for their roles in the growth platforms. For example, the acquisition in 2003 of Britain's Amersham added diagnostic pharmaceuticals and life sciences to GE Medical Systems's imaging equipment and software arsenal, creating what GE says is the world's most comprehensive medical diagnostic company. Now called GE

Healthcare, the business will be headquartered in London. The acquisition of Universal Vivendi positioned NBC as a media company with vast reach and growth potential.

A new organization structure divides the businesses into "growth engines," such as health care and finance, and "cash generators" such as insurance and equipment services. Many businesses in these groupings are recombinations of old GE businesses. Among growth engines, for example, transportation is composed of the former aircraft and rail businesses, and infrastructure combines parts of the old industrial systems and specialty materials units. This division into new categories has also brought a subtle but important change in reporting. Where before all of GE's business reported to the CEO, now the cash generators are in the hands of seasoned executives who take full responsibility for them. This gives Immelt more time to focus on the growth business, which report directly to him.

In the operating and people elements, Immelt is gearing up to generate as much organic growth as possible, because he believes it's the best way to create long-term value. His approach bases GE's differentiation on a combination of technological leadership and intense customer focus. Immelt is continuing the well-established Six Sigma initiative and putting heavy emphasis on digitization and At the Customer, For the Customer (described in Chapter 10). In the people element, he's focusing on identifying and developing growth leaders skilled in the application of technology who are able as well to focus on customers and help customers prosper. He's also linking compensation—including his own—to revenue growth and cash generation targets, as well as to GE's stock performance in relation to the S&P 500 over a five-year period.

In two years, Immelt has accomplished a profound yet controlled and sharply focused transformation of an iconic institution. We'd sum him up as a bold, business savvy leader able to look around corners and courageous enough to take all measures necessary to adjust his business model to a changing environment. And we'd assert that this sort of courage–to redo your predecessor's business model or even the one you created yourself at some point in the past–is what will increasingly separate winners from losers in coming years.

■ ■ ■

AFTER MAKING A DECISION to change, you must be tough enough to follow through. This means facing up to wrenching choices about people and resources, some of which will undoubtedly cause you emotional pain: the guy in whom you'd put so much stock clearly isn't up to handling the new challenge; the project you initiated yourself nine months ago now has no place in the business going forward.

People will resist for all sorts of reasons, and it takes strength to stay the course–especially when protests are vocal and emotional. Often you've got to be creative in forcing change without destroying the people you're trying to change. We know a division leader in a manufacturing company whose change initiative was in danger of falling on its face because he couldn't get two units to work collaboratively. He repeatedly brought the unit managers into his office and lectured them about the need to cooperate. They'd agree heartily, leave the office–and nothing would change.

These were good leaders, and the division head liked them both. But finally, as a last resort he took a gamble. He called them in for the umpteenth meeting, and this time he laid it on the line. He said, "You know, I'm going to have to fire you both. We've been good friends for all these years, and I appreciate all you've done. But I can't do this job if we can't get this cooperation, and you guys have proven you don't want to do it. Now, I have nice severance packages for both of you." He handed them their packages (which were indeed quite generous), reiterated that they'd done excellent work individually, gave them his heartfelt best wishes for the future, and closed the door behind them.

The two men were back in his office at six in the evening. "Look, we can work this out," they told him. "Well, that's wonderful," said our friend. "Now, let's do this. I'm going to take these packages and put them right here in the drawer. If you haven't worked this thing out in three to six months, I'm going to give them back to you. And I'm not going to call you every day, because you know you should do this." That was the last time he had to worry about them: they buried their differences and—while they never learned to like each other a lot—they did what had to be done.

That wasn't quite the end of the story. The two managers took the lesson they'd learned from our friend and used it to transform attitudes in their own historically antagonistic organizations. Within a year, the change initiative had substantially increased both revenues and profits for the whole division.

DRIVING REALISM IN THE ORGANIZATION

A leader can't confront reality if her organization as a whole doesn't. As we noted in Chapter 1, it's basic human behavior for many, if not most, people to deny reality, and embrace unreality, when the reality is more than they can bear. Business is no exception, despite the tendency of businesspeople to consider themselves uncommonly realistic. People get in the habit of finding ways to confirm their own thinking, which in time create barriers to seeing the realities that differ from those they're comfortable with.

Perversely, unreality is often the consequence of time-honored good leadership practices. One, which we mentioned earlier, is the counsel of like-minded people. Leaders develop teams and cadres whom they can trust to carry out their plans. Then they come to a crossroad or an inflection point. They turn to their teams for ideas, and because they're both busy and confident in the judgment of their teams, they accept the input without questioning it very closely. The same dynamics prevail down through the ranks: everybody is relying, to a greater or lesser degree, on the proven experience of others.

This is how organizations develop blind spots that lead them down the wrong paths in times of change. But the price of unreality-as-usual is rising all the time, and fighting it must now be a leadership priority. Nobody's going to ever create an organization where people are 100 percent realistic all the time, but the goal has to be to get as close as possible. And as we will see, there are proven ways to do that.

The more successful the business, ironically, the more likely it is to have such blind spots. After all, when the people running the business are doing splendidly, who wouldn't look for more of the same to hire and promote? And the longer the run of success, the harder it tends to be to change that mindset. Leaders who haven't confronted failure are vulnerable to the unrealistic view that they know all they need to know. That's why Detroit took decades to get real about the changes in its competitive environment that began in the late 1960s. It's why an outsider—like Lou Gerstner at IBM—is sometimes needed to turn the *Titanic* away from the iceberg.

The job starts with straight talk at the top: A leader can't expect realism from others without setting the example herself.

■ ■ ■

I WAS KNOWN TO BE FRANK, and by some, blunt. But I never saw any benefit in mincing words, because I knew it was important to force people to look realistically at themselves and their situations. Whether I was talking about the prospects of a given business or delivering a performance appraisal, the listener would get my unvarnished and realistic view.

Sometimes this meant stepping up to the front lines and taking hostile fire. When we had to close plants, I knew that the decision would inflict a lot of pain on a lot of people. But I felt the workers at the plant ought to be the first to know of the decisions, and the company's leaders always delivered the message personally. We'd gather the plant leadership, and together we told people what was going to happen and why, and that we would make sure that they were treated as fairly and respectfully as possible.

Similarly, when Honeywell had a wage freeze, some of my associates suggested that we should not make an official announcement but just stop giving people raises. I vetoed that. It would have spread by word of mouth anyway, and we wouldn't have had the chance to explain why we were doing it.

■ ■ ■

TALKING STRAIGHT ALSO MEANS that you are realistic in the plans you make and the goals you set. Start by being clear about your organization's own culture and capabilities. Many CEOs who describe their cultures in glowing terms are talking about what they'd like it to be, not necessarily what it is. They'll dwell on the positive parts of attitude surveys, and ignore the responses that raise troubling questions.

Granted, sometimes a leader has to transcend the existing reality in order to inspire people to reach beyond. That's the reason for stretch goals: they challenge people to surpass limitations that seem based in reality but which often are only habitual or self-imposed. But even stretch goals have to be anchored in realism. You may be convinced that your people can do more than they think they can do, but you'd better make sure you've judged their capabilities correctly. Ask yourself: If I put this challenge out there, will we actually have the ability to meet it? Do we have the resources, including the human capabilities?

Straight talk should be part of all communications to internal and external constituencies. CEOs are often coached on how to slant their message for the investment community, employees, or the board. How can that be straight talk? The message should be one and the same, reflecting your grasp of the business model, the reasons underlying it, and the linkages between externalities, financial goals, strategy, people, and organization. Coaches can help make the communication more cogent and improve the choice of words, but the basic message should come directly from your thoughts, which must be crisp and consistent.

The message must also be clear and simple. Way too much corporate communication is overly complex. Sometimes this is a ego play: the communicator wishes to show that he understands things that you can't possibly grasp. But often it's because the idea hasn't been thought through sufficiently. One of the great leadership arts is reducing complexity to its simplest expression without being simplistic.

The clear, simple message should be repeated often. Most of us tend to assume that once we've said something, it's over and done with. Not so: it takes repetition, sometimes ad nauseam, to persuade everybody in an organization that the leader means what she's saying and that what she's saying needs to be taken seriously.

An organization is only as good as the quality of its dialogues, from those in meetings to the informal exchanges where many, if not most, decisions are nurtured and shaped. If the dialogues are not candid and forthright, unfiltered and uncorrupted by political agendas, realism will never be surfaced. And while the leader's example is critical for establishing a baseline of realism in dialogue, it's not enough by itself. We can only reiterate here what we developed at length in our book *Execution*: robust dialogue has to be nurtured by both example and intervention, and reinforced with rewards for those who practice it and penalties for those who don't.

IDENTIFYING AND DEVELOPING THE RIGHT KIND OF LEADERS

The generalities of leadership development are well documented (we've had some things to say about it ourselves previously), and we won't attempt to provide any kind of comprehensive guide. But we do need focus on the specifics of recognizing and developing leaders who can confront reality.

Even the best processes for identifying and developing leaders are no guarantee of success. People fail for any number of reasons. They may get overwhelmed, feeling that they're in over their head, and lose self-confidence. They may think they've arrived and decide they can relax.

Some leaders drop by the wayside because their talents and skills aren't equal to the demands of the new job. A very few simply stumble into the kind of bad luck that nobody can control. Then, of course, there is the inexplicable. At one company we know, a CEO candidate had gone through the utmost scrutiny before being hired. But when he got the top job, something happened to change him. He fell apart psychologically and wrote himself a check for a large amount of money. No one who knew him could have seen that coming.

The processes most companies use to spot potential leaders aren't geared to finding those with the qualities needed most today. First, as we pointed out earlier in this chapter, the traditional criteria are not very useful. We've made the case for leadership traits we think are important now and are likely to continue to be important as long as the world remains complex and fast changing. These include the qualities that comprise business savvy—in particular, the ability to see the totality of a business through the lens of the business model—and the intense curiosity that drives the need to know. Add to these several other items to look for. Does the person have the flexibility of mind, perpetual adaptability, willingness to change, and courage to risk failure that will drive a search for unique solutions? Does the person demonstrate the ability to envision jobs several levels higher and see his or her own job in that broader context? Does the person have a sound enough ego to recognize the limits of his or her knowledge or experience?

Once the criteria are spelled out, they of course need to be incorporated into the business's formal evaluation criteria. But as we explained in *Execution,* these HR-driven procedures are often highly imperfect. You also need to bring your own judgment–the perspective of the line leader–to the job. This requires that you carefully observe your developing leaders in action.

What does the person you're watching talk about in business meetings? What sparks her curiosity? How broad is her scope? Does she have a natural tendency to search for root causes? Does she shape a set of options before she does anything? Looking at the options is better than saying "I know exactly how to fix this," because many times the single solution is not the best.

You can learn a lot about a person by watching how he solves problems. Does he diagnose a situation based on what's worked in the past, resorting to familiar solutions, or does he search for new and creative approaches? We see too many people being groomed for the top who are great at building on the business models or initiatives of others but lack the ability or fortitude to set their own course and try new things. These are the people who, when they get the top job, will play defense and protect their paychecks until they have to leave.

You can gather insights in a classroom setting. At Honeywell's training facility, for example, it was routine to keep an eye on the three or four people who seemed to perform best in the class. You can also pick the up-and-comers out of the crowd by listening closely to what they talk and ask about in meetings.

Are the people you're looking at broad thinkers? Listen to the options they propose. You get a sense of their scope and range. Look, too, at whether they sit on those options or act on them. Some people will see three solutions, then let months pass before making a decision. Some will identify three solutions, then talk with other people, sift through them, select one, and go do it. Those are the kinds of people who deserve your further focus.

Seeing people in both up periods and down periods is an important test of how well they will deal with reality. You're looking for people who can perform successfully in both conditions. If a person has had nothing but successes, you can't know how she's going to behave when things turn sour.

Many companies' leadership-development processes fail to produce the right kind of leaders because they skip some critical aspects of bringing along their "high potentials." The fast track *is* often too fast, omitting work experiences that would have prepared and tested leadership candidates. The idea of moving people from business to business or function to function is a good one; it gets them to grow beyond their narrow specialties. But the typical quick rotation doesn't allow results to catch up with the person. Without adequate evaluation and follow-through, it is no more than a ticket-punching exercise. Maybe that's why we've recently seen so many seasoned executives, people who earned their stripes through years of success, being called back to active duty.

One useful developmental tool is a stretch assignment— one that is more challenging than the individual's experience suggests that he can handle, but which you suspect may reveal hidden potential. Often these assignments have to be created to give the person a particular kind of experience—such as running a product line or a customer segment, or working in a function completely different from the person's career track. These have to be legitimate jobs that put people to the test early in their careers and force them to utilize the business model.

Perhaps the biggest flaw in traditional development programs is that often nobody's paying the right kind of attention to the developing leaders. Whether they make their numbers is just part of what you need to know. The real question is not whether they got the job done but *how* they got the job done. You need to watch them carefully as they progress over time—do you see them not just doing good jobs but growing in more challenging assignments? What are they doing to enhance their skills—reading, seminars, what else? Good, progressive people are always learning more about things. Do they search for and listen to different points of view?

Leaders with growth potential should receive some kind of education on specific topics like ethics or strategy or business model construction. Sports and the military do a great job with this sort of training, but we don't see the same rigor in sifting, sorting, and stretching people in business organizations. Johnson & Johnson, GE, and Honeywell are among the exceptions. Honeywell had good results with simulations, where groups of people take opposing sides on a business issue, develop their cases, and then debate their conclusions. Structured correctly, such an exercise trains people in thinking beyond their own views.

At every stage of their development, evaluate your up-and-comers rigorously. You're counting on them to grow, and you have to continually reevaluate their growth potential. For those on a fast track, this means a comprehensive, two-day assessment that yields a detailed, ten- to fifteen-page report. Looking at these assessments, you can see whether you're matching the right people to the right jobs. You also need to be sure they hear about what they do well and not so well. Everyone deserves feedback, but the people you single out deserve more frequent and more strenuous feedback.

A mentor or coach can be very helpful in providing candid appraisals. Many individuals out there are great coaches. They often play second fiddle to those who are more conspicuous—say, the customer-contact guy, or another person who makes a visible contribution to the organization. As a leader, you need to spot those individuals, make sure their talents are put to the best use, and reward them commensurately.

A well-focused process for identifying and developing the right leadership qualities will greatly raise the odds that those you advance will be up to the job of confronting today's business realities.

Conclusion

Letter to Jane: On Confronting Reality for Growth and Opportunity

Dear Jane:

We enjoyed our conversation with you last week and came away impressed with the amount of progress you've achieved with your business in the last two years.

As you well know, improvements in operating margins resulted from a more cost-effective manufacturing approach and good discipline in containing or eliminating nonessential "general and administrative" expenditures. Seeing your customer satisfaction index and market share soar is proof positive of a superb managerial performance.

Yet we share your concerns about the future of the business. Given the growth potential of the market you serve, it's not surprising that others are moving aggressively to be a part of it. Therefore, despite all you and your team have accomplished, you have an even bigger challenge ahead. It is clear from our discussion and the work that you have done on your business model that your environment is about to undergo substantial change.

As we understand it, one of your competitors has recently been granted a patent for a technology that is expected to produce a product at a cost 40 percent below your largest and highest margin offering. As if this is not enough, you've got an unforeseen and aggressive new competitor entering, with substantial resources, a sizable distribution business, and a history of successfully penetrating markets new to them.

On the other hand, you're already ahead of the game: you recognize you've got a problem that won't yield to familiar solutions, and you're willing to undertake bold new actions. It is our experience that many business leaders encountering unexpected adversity have trouble confronting the reality of their environment. Rather than facing reality head-on, they tend to stay on the periphery and do what they've always done. It is appropriate to remind people in times like these that the cost of being late in responding can be horrendous, whereas the rewards for an early response can be enormous.

We learned the other day that you and your team have already framed responses to the following questions:

- Are the financial forecasts realistic given your current environment?

- Are the strategic plans and operating tactics clear and specific?

Conclusion

- Is your model differentiated from those of your competitors?

- Is the model easily and quickly adaptable to changing environments?

Your review of the financial history of your current competitor's offerings illustrates that the new differentiated product offered by your competitor will probably quickly gain share. So, Jane, the question centers on the most effective response.

Your current business model has dictated that you market a relatively selective product line through your own sales force directly to customers. This strategy has been helped by attractive growth in your served segments. However, the current circumstances suggest that you will need a new approach to remain highly successful.

We suggest that you construct a model that calls for offering a more diverse range of products, all derived from your current offerings and at different price points, to a broader customer base. As you examine your capabilities to execute this model, it will be apparent that you will need an augmented distribution capability. So include in your revised model the acquisition of a distribution and installation organization to help access the broader customer base. In addition to pulling through more product sales, you can develop a service capability heretofore ignored while at the same time providing some deterrent to the expected entry of the new competitor.

Once you've redone your business model to incorporate these changes, you will need to determine the new financial targets and begin to refine the necessary strategic actions and operating tactics necessary to execute your plan. You will then want to compare the new financial targets with the external realities and strategy and tactics to ensure your plan makes sense.

You'll doubtless find that you will have to iterate several times. And if the pieces still don't add up, you'll have to adjust the financial targets further. These may or may not meet all of your ambitions, but they will be realistic. That's the most important criterion of all.

Jane, we understand your concerns about leading your team in a very different direction from the one that has been so successful. But in our view you have no alternative, and, from a positive viewpoint, it provides a wonderful opportunity to reinvent your business.

As you proceed you will need to step back and judge whether you have the talent on your team that you will need for a successful mission. To begin with, you will need to address the fact that your team is entirely focused on a narrow product offering, and in order to make this plan work, you will need broader-based technologists and marketing people.

Then there's the question of how many of your people are ready for this major effort. From what you've told us, some are, but others are reluctant and defensive or resisting because they're stuck in the past. If you cannot convince the doubters to face the current circumstance, you will need to make some personnel changes. Do these now. We know how difficult this is to do, but putting off the painful decisions will waste time and money. Decisive action will provide confidence to your team.

We know the task is challenging. Some leaders would be overwhelmed by it. But it is clear from our conversations that you see the opportunity to put the company on a completely different track and to achieve an exciting competitive position.

And, of course, in the process you will demonstrate to your owners that you have the vision to understand forthcoming changes in your environment and the courage to do something proactive about them.

Jane, we have complete confidence in your ability to lead these changes. Move quickly, be positive, sensitive, and unrelenting. The time is now!

Holler if we can help!

Sincerely,
Ram & Larry

Notes

CHAPTER 1

1. Louis V. Gerstner, *Who Says Elephants Can't Dance?* (New York: HarperBusiness, 2002).

CHAPTER 2

1. "Linux Moves In on the Desktop, *Business Week*, February 23, 2004.

2. *The Economist*, "Survey, The World Economy," September 26, 2002; private sector debt data from Godley and Izurieta, the Levy Institute.

3. Ibid.

4. Board of Governors of the Federal Reserve System, Flow of Funds.

5. "Endless Bubbles," *U.S. Investment Perspectives*, Morgan Stanley Equity Research, June 23, 2003.

6. David Goldman, "Closed Economy? The World Is a Closed Economy!" *Wall Street Journal*, August 12, 2003.

7. Vincent Boland, "Banks Find a Way to Spread Their Risk," *Financial Times*, February 18, 2003.

8. *The Economist*, "Survey, The World Economy," September 26, 2002; private sector debt data from Godley and Izurieta, the Levy Institute.

9. Matthew Boyle, "Brand Killers," *Fortune*, July 21, 2003.

10. Terry Pristin, "Growth Spurt Accelerates in Wal-Mart's Backyard," *New York Times*, October 29, 2003.

11. Boyle, "Brand Killers."

12. Ibid.

Notes

13. U.S. Department of Commerce

14. Holman W. Jenkins: "Want More Deflation? Let's Go Hunting Cartels," *Wall Street Journal*, July 23, 2003.

15. "Verizon Bets Big on Cable," *Fortune*, May 31, 2004.

16. Ibid.

CHAPTER 3

1. Geoffrey Colvin, "A Concise History of Management Money," *Fortune*, June 28, 2004.

2. Nicholas G. Carr, *Does IT Matter?* (Cambridge: Harvard Business School Press, 2004), data from U.S. Department of Commerce.

3. Brian O'Reilly, "There's Still Gold in Them Thar Hills," *Fortune*, July 9, 2001.

4. Steve Lohr, "Bis Blue's Big Bet, Less Tech, More Touch," *New York Times*, January 25, 2004.

CHAPTER 6

1. Fred Vogelstein, "Can Cisco Dig Out of Its Hole?" *Fortune*, December 3, 2003.

2. Jim Kerstetter, "Sun Peeks Out of the Shadows," *BusinessWeek*, February 4, 2004.

3. Fred Vogelstein, "Scott McNealy's Lonely Battle Against Eternal Night," *Fortune*, October 13, 2003.

CHAPTER 9

1. Amy Koves, "How First Call Became No. 1," *Fortune*, June 21, 1999.

2. Todd Datz, "Merrill Lynch's Billion Dollar Bet," *CIO Magazine*, September 15, 2003.

3. Sami Kassab, Sector Note, *Professional Publishing*, October 2003.

CHAPTER 10

1. Andrew S. Grove, *Only the Paranoid Survive* (New York: Doubleday Currency, 1996).

Notes

2. George Anders, "The Top Ten Trends in Ten Industries," *Wall Street Journal,* February 9, 2004.

CHAPTER 12

1. Louis V. Gerstner, *Who Says Elephants Can't Dance?* (New York: Harper Business, 2002).

Acknowledgments

We are indebted to a great many people for their help in shaping this book and the ideas behind it.

We have benefited for nearly four decades, in more ways than we can describe, from the innumerable CEOs, directors, and executives who shared their experiences with us. We especially value the many we've worked with over long periods of time, allowing us to observe the origins, development, and outcomes of both their successes and failures. They provided us not just with snapshots of business reality, but with full-length documentary movies. They continue to force us to think and act on confronting reality. To all of these business leaders, we give our deepest thanks.

In the highly stimulating task of creating a book, Charlie Burck has been a tremendously helpful collaborator. Charlie is an *agent provocateur*, incessantly asking questions and driving to pin down the underlying logic behind our observations. He's the editor of editors; his work makes the work of the authors accessible to readers, and at the same time extremely useful. We are deeply grateful to him.

Our continuing journey with John Mahaney, our editor at Crown Business, is a constant source of inspiration. John has an unmatched ability to quickly conceive a project, and his eyes are constantly on the consumer: how will this book

Acknowledgments

help not only the CEO but also everyone from the business unit manager to the gas station owner? Nothing but the best suffices to satisfy his curiosity. We love working with him, and thank him profoundly.

Geri Willigan came to the project when we needed her the most, and her insights and hard work were very valuable. Geri has an uncanny ability to cut through clutter with the sharp knife of logic, and she knows how to structure a verbal dialogue on a piece of paper. We are extremely grateful to her.

Charlie, John, and Geri made up an amazing team—a great gift to any pair of authors.

We also want to thank Shana Drehs, associate editor of Crown, for her contributions in getting *Confronting Reality* ready for publication and Ian Mahaney for help in research.

We conclude with thanks to three great heroines of this enterprise, and of our many other undertakings: Eunice Krawczuk, Larry's longtime assistant; and Cynthia Burr and Carol Davis, Ram's Delta Team in Dallas. It is literally true that this book would not have been possible without them. To Eunice, Cynthia, and Carol: you have our boundless gratitude.

L.B.
R.C.

Index

Index

Index

Index

Index

Index

Index

About the Authors

LARRY BOSSIDY is the retired chairman of the board and CEO of Honeywell International Inc., a global $24 billion advanced technology, controls, and manufacturing company.

Mr. Bossidy's distinguished five-decade career in business began when he joined the General Electric Company's renowned financial training program in 1957. For the next thirty-four years, Mr. Bossidy served in a number of executive and financial positions with GE. He was chief operating officer of General Electric Credit Corporation (now GE Capital Corporation) from 1979 to 1981, executive vice president and president of GE's Services and Materials Sector from 1981 to 1984, and vice chairman and executive officer of General Electric Company from 1984 to July 1991.

Mr. Bossidy left GE in 1991 to join AlliedSignal Inc. as its chairman and CEO. He is credited with transforming Allied-Signal into one of the world's most admired companies. Many observers suggest that success was largely driven by Mr. Bossidy's intense focus on relentlessly executing growth, management development, and Six Sigma–based productivity initiatives. During his tenure with AlliedSignal, the company achieved consistent growth in earnings and cash flow, highlighted by thirty-one consecutive quarters of earnings-per-share growth of 13 percent or more and an eightfold appreciation of the company's share price. A number of senior executives who served under him are now CEOs of major companies.

In 1999, Mr. Bossidy became chairman of Honeywell International Inc., following the historic merger of AlliedSignal and Honeywell in December 1999. He retired from the company as scheduled in April 2000.

Honeywell's board of directors brought back Mr. Bossidy on July 3, 2001, as chairman and CEO of Honeywell International Inc., to stabilize the company following General Electric's prolonged and unsuccessful attempt to acquire Honeywell. Mr. Bossidy's second term focused on reinvigorating Honeywell's core management processes and improving its operations and cost structures.

Mr. Bossidy is coauthor of the best selling book *Execution: The Discipline of Getting Things Done,* a primer on effective hands-on leadership in today's competitive business environment. *Execution* has been translated into nineteen languages. Copies in print number more than 700,000 in the United States and more than 1.5 million copies worldwide. Since its publication in June 2002, *Execution* was consistently ranked on the *Wall Street Journal, New York Times,* and *BusinessWeek* business bestseller lists.

In 1993, Mr. Bossidy led the efforts of the U.S. business community to successfully secure congressional approval of the North American Free Trade Agreement. He was named CEO of the Year by *Financial World* magazine in 1994 and chief executive of the Year by *CEO Magazine* in 1998.

Mr. Bossidy, who graduated from Colgate University in 1957 with a BA degree in economics, is a member of the board of directors of JP MorganChase, Merck & Company, and Berkshire Hills Bancorp Inc. He is also an advisor to Aurora Capital Group, a leveraged buyout firm.

Mr. Bossidy was born in Pittsfield, Massachusetts. He and his wife, Nancy, have nine children.

About the Authors

RAM CHARAN is a highly sought after business advisor and speaker famous among senior executives for his uncanny ability to solve their toughest business problems. For more than thirty-five years, Dr. Charan has worked behind the scenes with top executives at some of the world's most successful companies, including GE, Verizon, Novartis, Dupont, Thomson, Honeywell, KLM, Bank of America, Home Depot, and Johnson Electric Hong Kong. He has shared his insights with many others through teaching and writing.

Dr. Charan's introduction to business came early while working in the family shoe shop in the small Indian village where he was raised. He earned an engineering degree in India and soon after took a job in Australia and then in Hawaii. When his talent for business was discovered, Dr. Charan was encouraged to pursue it. He earned MBA and doctorate degrees from Harvard Business School, where he graduated with high distinction and was a Baker Scholar. After receiving his doctorate degree, he served on the Harvard Business School faculty.

Dr. Charan is well known for providing advice that is down to earth and relevant and that takes into account the real-world complexities of business. Among his recommendations for achieving profitable growth, for example, are to search for "singles and doubles" as well as home runs and to develop what he calls a "growth budget" to instill discipline on growth initiatives. Identified by *Fortune* as the leading expert in corporate governance, Dr. Charan is helping boards go beyond the requirements of Sarbanes-Oxley and the New York Stock Exchange by providing practical ways to improve their group dynamics. Boards, CEOs, and senior-most human resource executives often seek his advice on talent planning and key hires.

Many people have come to know Dr. Charan through in-house executive education programs. His energetic, interactive teaching style has won him several awards. He won the Bell Ringer award at GE's famous Crotonville Institute and best teacher award at Northwestern. He was among *Business-Week*'s top ten resources for in-house executive development programs.

Over the past decade, Dr. Charan has captured his business insights in numerous books and articles. In the past five years, Dr. Charan's books have sold more than 1 million copies. These include the bestseller *Execution: The Discipline of Getting Things Done,* coauthored with Larry Bossidy, *What the CEO Wants You to Know, Boards at Work,* and *Every Business Is a Growth Business.* His book *Profitable Growth* was released by Crown Business in January 2004, and *Boards That Deliver* is forthcoming in January 2005. A frequent contributor to *Fortune,* Dr. Charan has written two cover stories, "Why CEOs Fail" and "Why Companies Fail." His other articles have appeared in the *Financial Times, Harvard Business Review, Director's Monthly,* and *Strategy and Business.*

Dr. Charan has served on the Blue Ribbon Commission on Corporate Governance and was elected a Fellow of the National Academy of Human Resources. He is on the board of Austin Industries. Dr. Charan is based in Dallas, Texas.

CHARLES BURCK is a writer and editor who collaborated with Ram Charan and Noel Tichy on their book *Every Business Is a Growth Business* and with Larry Bossidy and Ram Charan on *Execution: The Discipline of Getting Things Done.* Earlier in his career he was a writer and editor with *Fortune* magazine. He lives in New Orleans.